Data, Now Bigger and Better!

Data, Now Bigger and Better!

Edited and with an Introduction by
Tom Boellstorff and Bill Maurer

PRICKLY PARADIGM PRESS
CHICAGO

Prickly Paradigm Press, LLC
5629 South University Avenue
Chicago, IL 60637

www.prickly-paradigm.com

ISBN: 9780984201068
LCCN: 2014949663

Printed in the United States of America on acid-free paper.

Contents

Introduction

Tom Boellstorff and Bill Maurer

This pamphlet brings together five authors responding to current debates regarding the new salience of big data in society. By big data, we refer to the mobile and digital computational systems that permit the large-scale generation, collection, and analysis of information about people's and devices' activities, locations, and transformations. We refer as well to as the social and technical effects of those systems and data, and the speculative hype, hopes, and futures that accompany them. While our individual responses address different aspects of these debates, four guiding principles link them together.

First, we challenge the strong tendency for discussions regarding digital technology to be shaped by obsessions with "trending." The value of an analysis becomes measured by claims about the future rather than accuracy in explaining the past or present. From public health to climatology, trying to predict the future is not always wrongheaded—it is good to act on signals indicating the outbreak of a disease, or to model what might happen to coastal cities as more carbon is dumped into the air. But with regard to the matter at hand, focusing on the unknowable often diverts critical attention from the emerging present. This is, for instance, why we refer to "big data" in this pamphlet, despite attempts by many commentators to claim the phrase is already antiquated. In our view the planned obsolescence of terminology leads to term-coinage standing in for insight. No term ever perfectly captures its referent. "Big data" helpfully denotes a set of sociotechnological facts and connotes an atmosphere of simultaneous hype and legitimate innovation that represents the subject of our collective inquiry.

Second, we challenge the cultures of expertise that characterize discussions of big data. The move to data is often characterized as a move away from narrative, from ethnography, from the qualitative and interpretive. But as many coders and number-crunchers themselves assert, we cannot treat data as a purely quantitative phenomenon. Our analyses are interpretive and critical in character, yet shaped by a range of deep engagements with data. We are located in both academia and industry, and see the complicities and collaborations that emerge from that double location as a source of conceptual strength.

Third, all of our contributions to this pamphlet draw on anthropological perspectives, but not specifically ethnographic ones. As Tim Ingold has argued in his aptly titled article "Anthropology Is Not Ethnography," sociocultural anthropology is more than a basket of ethnographic methods like participant observation and interviewing. The value of anthropology lies also in its conceptual frameworks, frameworks that are comparative as well as field-based. These theoretical contributions of anthropology date back more than a century, and turning to these classic debates provides an effective counter to the future-oriented hype and speculation so characteristic of discussions regarding big data. In this pamphlet, names like Malinowski, Lévi-Strauss, and Mauss appear as centrally as those of present-day thinkers. Discussions of kinship, exchange, and even cooking shape our analyses.

Fourth, our contributions are shaped by what our colleague Carl DiSalvo has termed "speculative civics"—which in his analysis links the emphasis on unknowable futures mentioned above with the emergence of entrepreneurialism and precarity in a public life shaped by data technologies not always open to scrutiny. The public is important, in both its classic and its newly emergent political senses. This is why we attend to activists like Edward Snowden and public intellectuals like Jaron Lanier, as well as broader debates over the nature of data and the meaning of "economy."

Through these guiding principles, we seek to contribute to a vitally important debate over the relationship between data, power, and meaning in the contemporary world. Big data experts often speak of the "three Vs" when characterizing crucial parameters for understanding what makes data "big": volume, variety, and velocity. In our view, "three Rs" might prove more significant: relation, recognition, and rot. We emphasize how data is formed through relations that extend beyond "data" itself; how what counts as data (and data's referent) is a social process with political overtones; and that data is always in real-time transformation in ways that cut across notions of nature and culture. Geoffrey Bowker and Lisa Gitelman remind us, to quote the title of the latter's recent book, that *"Raw Data" Is An Oxymoron* (2013). But like fruit and food, data can be transformed by decomposition as much as by "cooking it up" for analysis.

Our pamphlet begins with Genevieve Bell's "The Secret Life of Big Data." Drawing on her experiences as an anthropologist and Vice President & Intel Fellow at Intel Labs, Bell playfully anthropomorphizes and personalizes "big data" so as to unpack its meanings and implications from an anthropological perspective. In the chapters that follow, each author builds from Bell's provocations to explore aspects of big data through the guiding principles discussed above.

Nick Seaver explores claims that big data will submerge other modes of social inquiry, invoking Chris Anderson's influential argument that the "data deluge" renders qualitative research and critical theory moot. To do so, he turns to other moments when computational formalism seemed to overwhelm social analysis, from Bronislaw Malinowski's criticisms of the "bastard algebra" that kinship studies in anthropology had become by 1930, to Clifford Geertz's complaints against the cognitive anthropologists of the 1960s and 1970s. Seaver then draws on the work of Marilyn Strathern to examine how the very ways in which methods are taken to "relate" (in both a cognitive and kinship sense) have consequences for anthropological analysis and knowledge production more broadly.

Mel Gregg begins from the observation that the word "data" in English derives from the same Latin root as "gift," "that which is given." But, of course, data are never given in advance. Asking "what is big" and "what is data" pose problems of scale, scope, the epistemological claims involved in all the hype about big data—hype which often takes the form of visual representations, infographics and the like. Gregg develops notions like "data sweat" to explore data's agency, porosity, and relation to social and ecological environments of data "trash" and "exhaust." She reminds us, too, that the colonial impulse in big data's technological infrastructures, conditions of production and modes of knowledge mean that the gift never comes for free.

Bill Maurer takes up the internet guru and critic Jaron Lanier's call for a new economy of big data, one that would reward people for the collection and use of "their" data. While Lanier's proposal is compelling, Maurer argues that it sidelines key questions regarding the nature of property and person, issues of longstanding anthropological concern. Drawing an analogy with the dawn of new reproductive technologies, Maurer asks whether we are witnessing a similar new kind of birth. He extends this line of thinking by drawing on the anthropological canon of kinship and exchange theory, asking what other relationships come into view if we treat "big data" as party to a marriage exchange, and complicate the gifts we imagine data brings with some of the bastard algebra Seaver dissects.

Tom Boellstorff seeks to open a conversation regarding the theoretical frameworks that shape the notion of "big data," despite the fact that the very term is often taken to imply a pre-theoretical or even non-theoretical perspective on the world. In his chapter (a substantially revised version of an essay that appeared in the journal *First Monday* in October 2013), Boellstorff first explores the history of the notion of "data," but also the way in which a sense of being "dated" haunts the study of internet-related technology and society.

He then turns to the notion of "metadata," showing how distinctions between data and metadata are social (and political) rather than a priori. He then develops the notion of "the dialectic of surveillance and recognition" to examine how social relationships to big data are shaped by desire as well as fear. Finally, he reframes the distinction between "raw data" and "cooked data" by introducing notions of "rotted data" and "thick data."

Our collaboration is shaped by a dense network of social and intellectual relationships stretching back two decades, but made possible in its current incarnation by the Intel Science and Technology Center for Social Computing (ISTC-Social). The ISTC-Social is an example of some of the new collaborations anthropologists are forging in hybrid industrial-academic settings. Bill Maurer and Scott Mainwaring have written for the *Journal of Business Anthropology* about the odd economic and intellectual configurations that brought the ISTC-Social into being. But this pamphlet is not "about" the collaboration so much as a demonstration of what such a venture can do. We thank in particular Paul Dourish for his support and insights in that regard, and have found the conversations and collaborations made possible by this center to have helped us advance the arguments we make throughout this pamphlet.

The Secret Life of Big Data

Genevieve Bell

"Big data" occasions a big question: How do we start talking about the socio-technical imagination? How do we even begin, given that technological history is littered with countless space-age visions for the future just around the corner that never came to pass? It is a perilous time to think about big data: business interest is at a peak, but has it already crested? Popular debate hovers between concerns over privacy and government snooping, and indifference about the surrender of vast quantities of information just by turning on one's phone. The very term big data may well disappear by the time you read this pamphlet, much as the prefix "cyber" to refer to anything internet is quickly vanishing.

There are big arguments about how to define big data. It is also already occupying a huge place in the landscape of what technology is, what it might offer, and what it could be. When this chapter was still a spoken lecture I could remark, as if it were a new thing,

"We already see big data appearing in newspaper headlines." We're beyond the point where that generates surprise. Big data now bubbles up to the surface in all sorts of places. It is already finding its space in a cartography of social imagination. An advertisement for a technology company can sport a stylized street sign indicating we're at the corner of Big Data and the Cloud. At least for a certain market, big data literally points to a destination.

Of course as an anthropologist my first response to this moment is to ask, "yeah, but is it really new?" In 1085 A.D. William the Conqueror surveyed his empire and said, "I don't actually know what everyone is doing. Could you make me a list? I'd like to know what all the men in the kingdom are up to and how many sheep they have." The Domesday Book became an entire way of framing what it meant to be in England under William the Conqueror. It is effectively big data. It may not have been connected to the internet, but it was searchable. There were people who were custodians of that book. You could go to them and say, "I'm looking for men who have more than a 100 sheep and less than 200 sheep who haven't given me a lot of money this year." And there was someone whose job it was to run the algorithm on the data to find the men who fit that category. The Domesday Book involved three quite distinct things:

- The survey—which collected information, facts;
- The Winchester Roll—that was created out of the facts;
- The "day of judgment"—when taxes, ownership and military obligations were determined for hundreds of years to come.

Today's "big data" is made up of the same three things: facts (data), frameworks (visualizations and analytics) and extracted value (algorithms). The difference is the awe-inspiring scale made possible through computation.

Part of the Chinese government's invention of bureaucracy nearly two and a half thousand years ago was about creating a formulation for managing what was an ever-increasing trove of material. Its files have existed for hundreds if not at this point thousands of years. In this sense too, the notion of big sets of data is not new. The notion that those big sets of data might frame the way we think; how we are identified, how we identify ourselves—these ideas are not new. And, finally, macho talk about how big, fast and multitasking data can be: these ideas are as old as still dominant forms of Euro-American masculinity.

Our life is rich with data. Not all data is written down. Not all data is recorded in quite those senses, but for me here the push is to say what is the thing about all this information that we think is new? For me the issue is not scale or speed or variety. It lies else-where.

Will everything produce data?

One promise of big data is that everything is going to produce data. Cell phones will produce data, traffic lights will produce data, refrigerators will produce data, we will produce data, our bodies will produce data, our devices will produce data. There start to be some inter-esting questions. What does that data look like? Will in fact everything produce data? Will we *let* everything produce data? Just because you can connect a toaster to the internet doesn't necessarily mean we want to have its data. There are a lot of reasons why that might not be a useful thing or why, on the other hand, it might be potentially a very useful thing.

The first analytical question I would like to pose about big data is how do we understand the framing of a popular argument in the tech community that says that *everything will be or will produce data*? What does that mean about the notion of production, about notions of objects and subjects, and about notions of data? A future in which everything is "connected" and producing data is both overwhelming and spectacularly interesting. It signals both serious plenitude and networked singularity.

Will everyone produce data?

Similarly, what does it mean to suggest everyone will produce data, or even to ask the question: will everyone produce data? We live in a world where the internet and it forms of connectivity are remarkably unevenly distributed. This is due to politics and economics: the pricing structures of the internet are different in different places. Certain governments regulate the internet in different ways, in terms of content, availability, appropriate forms of activity, appropriate in-points. The adoption of devices is remarkably different in different places in the hands of different people. It is also due to infrastructure: in some places the internet is strongly gated for downloads versus uploads. Undersea cables move data at different rates between different countries.

There are already hot spots of data production and then big vast empty gaps. Some people are producing more data than others. Some data appear to be from one human organism, but it may actually be from a whole collection of people. I once had it explained to me in no uncertain terms by fairly passionate big data sponsors that the more data there would be, the more truth we would have. The more truth we would have, the more we would know. Everyone would produce data, thus we would understand everyone better.

It's relatively easy to point out that the ways that data is produced, coded and understood is always being read through a series of cultural lenses, whether they are visible or not. Who has agency to produce data, who has agency to control data, who even knows if there is data out there about them? These are the basic questions for an ethnography of big data. But that's obvious.

What if you could go do fieldwork among the Big Data, if you could track down some big data and have a semi-structured interview and a bit of back and forth—where would the conversation get you? That ethnographic interview might end up much more interesting than some of the stories we are starting to tell now.

What does data want?
And what is wanted from it?

I want to ask, after Philip K. Dick: If data were thinking would it have wishes? Or after Freud, What does data want? As I've already mentioned, many in the business say, "more data." Data wants more data, and if more data wants even more data then soon all that data wants an algorithm and then several algorithms. Big data wants accumulation of more of itself. If this is true, then the question becomes: what is it about this particular historical moment that makes so compelling the need to return to an empirical point of view? What is going right now that makes us say we need data, more and more and more of it? What is the anxiety, the fear, the instability, the place that the world has moved in such a way that the thing that we think will be *comforting*, although we would never use that language, is more data. Why is this so comforting and so seductive, or, why is it that this is the moment in which more data seduces? Dissatisfaction with or disavowal of ideology is itself ideological, after all.

Data keeps it real

The possibility of accumulating ever more data depends on people understanding it as virtual—its virtuality permits its infinity. Yet a whole lot of data has physical manifestations and physical representations. In a temple in Pusan, South Korea, many people after praying leave behind small plastic Buddhas. They used to leave wooden ones, and they used to leave many other things besides. I asked why, and people told me, "I need to make it real that I've been here. I want to leave something behind." There is something here about the hope, the prayer, the wish being physically manifested in an object.

Not all data is going to be invisible. Some data is going to be physically represented in objects. Some data wants to be an object. Some data wants to be objectified. I suspect that some data doesn't want to be invisible. Because when you are physically there you are much more of a pain in the ass.

Data loves a good relationship

Most data doesn't exist in isolation. Data really likes being in relationships. Not all of those relationships are immediately visible.

As a human being engaged in anything on the internet, chances are you have done something that is making someone or something that collects data absolutely crazy: you have more than one person logged into your Amazon account, more than one person uses your iTunes account, you are sharing your Netflix password with people who don't live in your house. Five of your friends go to a cybercafé every day and log on into the same account. You have a cell phone that you are sharing with a whole series of your colleagues. You are running a microenterprise in a train station in India, where you are servicing multiple clients and pirating content for all of them off a single account. At every single one of those points you look like an individual. You are someone who confuses the Amazon recommendation engine, because you like books on physics and Dora the Explorer and also sex toys. Occasionally Amazon will send you a note saying, in so many words, "I'm not exactly sure how this is working out, will you help me?" It wants more relationships in order to determine (who) you (are).

We all own devices that don't speak to each other, or don't speak very well to each other. We have any number of digital traces that don't actually connect except through our bodies. All the things we know about social power, hierarchy, notions of what talks to what, in what manner and why apply. The people who are coding data, writing algorithms, creating recommendation engines, are determining what kind of relationships there should be between data sets and making judgments about what data should speak to what other data. But the algorithms themselves draw in new data sets when they see them becoming available and have been pre-coded to want to make relations with them.

Data doesn't always have the best network

Not all data is created equal, because not all data is running on a 10 gigabyte Ethernet fiber (and even this technical reference may be dated by the time you read this!). Some of it is on a dial-up. Some of it is on things that are only occasionally connected to the internet. For data created in the United States to get to anywhere else, it has to run on undersea cables that are controlled by third parties, the speeds of which are regulated a year in advance. That data enters other countries through gates which in turn determine how fast that data is going to flow inside the network within the country, which in turn is determined by anything from a government regulator who proposes what the standard should be in terms of connectivity speeds, or a private entity determining how much you should pay per packet. Depending on the physical gateways that data is running through, some governments and private enterprises can have a look inside, creating even more data, and also determining what data does and doesn't flow on the network.

More to the point, not all data is created equal to flow on the network. Video moves differently than text. Photos move differently than sound. Television and content moves in a completely different formulation than all of those things. There are arguments about how the network has been architected and scaled that suggests that certain sorts of data are going to be more effective than others. Certain sorts of buildings, certain sorts of environments mean that some data gets around easier than others. If you live in an old Australian home you are effectively living in a Faraday Cage. They have metal roofs and metal struts to hold up a lot of stonework. It turns out they are terrible for Wi-Fi and Bluetooth. So if you are in one of those networks your happy little Fitbit data just doesn't run around quite the way you wish it did. If you are in Singapore it turns out your Fitbit data doesn't run quite the way you wish it did because it's raining 6 months of the year and it turns out that water occludes wireless signals.

So imagining all the data will move freely everywhere in a kind of universal moment of splendor may not be the case. Not to mention if you have an interest in stopping it, looking at it, moving it around, storing it, having a bit of a think before you (or a government, or a corporation) passes it on.

Data has a country

Data is also going to know where it came from. Data has a country. It is already produced under certain policy regimes. Medical information is created in a certain kind of way to comply with state regulations.

Data has things on its proverbial body that will tell us where it came from. Data is not a denatured subject—it is not the pinnacle of abstraction (a critique probably leveled against it by some anthropologists). There is also a whole series of different ways in which data can come from places. So—not just a country but a *style* of coming from a country. And if you know what you're looking for, you'll be able to see that place and those styles. There will be the clues and the traces of its country, its point of origin, the moment that it appeared. There may also be traces of its travels.

Data is feral

At the same time, data is going to have a capacity to defy the expectations of the places where it was created and traveled, and will start to have another life. It will be repurposed. Algorithms create new forms of data, and that data finds lives in unexpected places. Some of the data that is produced in one format will be used in a different one to do something completely different.

Data can already go feral and go wild. It can jump the fence and start roaming the countryside.

The history of technology is that most technology doesn't end up in the hands of the people it was anticipated for, doing the work it was anticipated to do. These unintended consequences usually tend to be very spectacular. Yet people imagine that we are going to connect data sets to the internet, that many devices are going to create data and that somehow all of that data is going to stay stunningly controlled and doing exactly what it is told. In the hands of a government this leads to fear of totalitarianism. In the hands of corporations it leads to coupons! And muted, if audible at all, political critique. But it is the stunning hubris of civilization that it imagines its domesticated animals won't some day go wild, that everything will stay behind the fence. I just cannot see a way in which, secretly, part of what data wants desperately is to get over the fence and get going.

Data has Responsibilities

In the community where I grew up, when people tell you a story about their country, about their family, about the things that happened there, they tell you that story knowing that that they make you part of the responsibility of telling that story properly the next time. They are the custodians of those stories, they are also the custodians of the responsibility of doing the right thing with those stories.

This is data that comes with responsibilities. Some of them clearly we can imagine will be legislative. "You know you cannot share these particular pieces of data. You cannot tell this particular thing." Some of the responsibilities I suspect will not be about shutting the conversation down, but about opening it up. If the notion is that some data is meant to be told, then other data probably has a story that isn't imperative. Still other data has the responsibility to be a part of a conversation, which might change its mind over the course of that conversation. What does that mean? What would it mean to architect a system where big data had responsibilities? Not that we had a responsibility to keep it safe, say, but that it had a serious of piece of work it needed to do, a story it was compelled to say.

Data keeps it messy but likes to look good

Data will resist being tidied up. Data will be messy. There will be data sets produced by the same person on parallel devices that look completely different from each other. There will be data produced on the same human being in the same moment that will suggest conflicting ideas that may reveal two completely different realities and truths. You know not all data is going to be clean. Not every data set is going to be full. Most data sets will in fact be partial at best; most likely deeply partial at worst. The temptation is going to be to constantly tidy up the data, to neaten up the data, to make it fit the algorithm. To make it fit the spreadsheet.

Data is also never going to be a complete set. It's always going to be messy. It is always in some ways going to be in this constant place of the attempt to impose cleanliness on it and the reality is that because most of this data is being either directly produced by human beings or produced by devices, services, and applications that were created by human beings and even the algorithms doing the work were ultimately created by human beings and even when the algorithms go feral and create their own algorithms those will all somewhere encode entanglements of human and non-human thought, assumptions, cognition, ideas, responsibilities, cultural practices. And all of those resist tidying up.

Data also lie in order to look good. We already know that people lie in constructing their data—their online dating profile, their Facebook page. Algorithms that clean data also bend the data toward being better looking than it really is. Does the algorithm lie?

Data doesn't last forever

Not all data wants to last forever. Some data would like to just go away. Some of us wish that it would go away faster than it will. There is a reason why applications like Snapchat became really popular. Snapchat allows people to share images and words but does not build an archive of those exchanges on its servers and does not permit storage on people's individual phones. Once it's sent, it's gone (at least: that's what everyone thought before it settled with the US Federal Trade Commission over its collection of personal data). Some applications make data ephemeral. Some of the stories we tell about ourselves and others are embedded in complicated calculations of time.

The aboriginal people I grew up with never call the name of someone who is dead, which means taking class rolls was always really complicated. So when my teachers used to take roll it would be, "Kumanjai, Kumanjai, Kumanjai, Genevieve, Kumanjai, Kumanjai, Sarah, Rachel, Kumanjai, Kumanjai," using names that had dropped out of circulation. Some name data had gone away.

Yet in the community I've spent the last 20 years in, people call every name. They call every name for 20 generations as a way of saying, this is who we are and where we come from. And so then you never want to take the name away. Two groups of people less than 1,000 kilometers apart with two completely different notions about what you keep and what you don't, about what needs to last forever and what needs to go away because it's just too hard to keep in the present world.

So what does it mean to imagine that not all data wants to last forever and that some data wants to be gone and then the incredible complication of us not always not wanting it to be gone? I want to call the names of the men who raised me and I can't; it's disrespectful. I know their names and I could say them out loud. What does it mean to imagine the data that's effectively unsayable? Or that just can't be said because it doesn't circulate in quite the same way?

What are the next questions?

If these are the things that data wants, it wants to be real, it wants a country and a responsibility, it's going to be feral, and messy. It's going to want to last forever and be ephemeral and tell lies and look good all at the same time. If those are the wants of data, what does that mean for us as a research community about what the critical questions are going forward?

For me there are three.

How to read an algorithm

We know how to think about activities, we know how to think about objects, we know how to think about texts: that's part of our critical vocabulary. I think a much harder part of our critical vocabulary is to interrogate the sense-making tools that sit on top of the data. So if we know how to be critical of data, do we know how to be critical of the sense-making tools?

One of the main forms that sense-making operates over big data is mechanized. It's an algorithm. They are in and of themselves cultural objects. But cultural objects that are a little hard for most of us to read in quite the ways we know how to read an object or a story. To read them as objects, as practices, as moments is more complicated than some of the ways we know how to read other things and it's going to require if not retooling, then certainly engagement with a different community. It's time to learn some math, some coding, and to actually engage with some programmers.

Studying the new priests and alchemists

The time has come to return to Laura Nader's point that we need to be studying up the system and not constantly down and across the system. There is a charge to imagine how to study communities of big data custodians, their communities of practice, the things that they are doing and their consequences.

I heard them recently called the priests and alchemists, a tipping of the hand to the fact that part of what was going on might not be entirely real. It was also pointed out to me that there were not only high priests and alchemists, but also quants and geeks, that you should trust the quants and the geeks even though near as I could tell they were exactly the same people as the priests and the alchemists, just in a different company and contexts. This suggests that they can be our collaborators, too: they're not always the same person or in the same position at the same time; like everyone, they are multiple.

And, by the way, these contexts include all the different regulatory frameworks. What will happen at the moment that for instance the EU regulates privacy and data ownership in a very particular way, and that particular way is not only at odds with how it is or isn't regulated in the United States, but actually in conflict? What will it mean when the data sets live in one place (perhaps due to statutory rule, perhaps due to happenstance of infrastructure) and the algorithm works from somewhere else? Or the data set and the algorithm are in the same building, but the data is going to move, or some of what that algorithm works on is illegal, is inappropriate, is unwanted?

Critiquing the (new) empiricism and countering it with our own

Someone said in a meeting I was at with technology investors: More facts are better; data is truth; more data equals more truth; if we have more data we can understand people better; and data equals humans. I referenced similar language earlier. But on this occasion, it was a bit too much for me. I had to pound the table and point out that there was no such thing as Truth. That was not the right thing to say to the Wall Street bankers, it turns out. One of them conceded that, yes, it was probably true that *some* data didn't equal truth, but *more* data absolutely equaled truth.

I began by asking why it is that the language around big data and its social-technical imaginary involves such a remarkable reassertion of empiricism. This reassertion is being made by some very influential voices with large megaphones (Chris Anderson being perhaps the loudest; see his contribution to *WIRED* in 2008, which Nick Seaver mentions in his contribution to this pamphlet). Let's not mince words: this reassertion represents the erasure of whole bodies of knowledge that many in the social sciences and humanities have argued for pretty aggressively for more than a century. But it's also only *one* kind of empiricism, and one that denies a lot of what's most interesting about big data: what big data wants, as I've tried to outline here.

Part of the work, as data moves from headlines to some of the things we study and some of the things we implement, is to bring our theoretical "A game" to this conversation. The theoretical tools that we don't always think of as needing to be re-rehearsed really need to be re-rehearsed, which is going to mean passionate conversations about all the things that to my mind have always mattered: gender, race, class, sexuality, history, nationality, and oh, by the way, *power* that runs through all of this. It's going to require theory as well as other empiricisms that try to stay true to the data, big or otherwise. But it's especially important as critical social scientists and humanists to stay true to the big data, too. Again, this is going to involve some retooling and making friends with the custodians and alchemists, geeks and quants.

If I sit in meetings and have people tell me that whoever has the biggest data set wins, you already know there is a whole set of conversations we should be having differently. And as soon as anyone asserts that data equals truth, you know there is a whole other set of conversations we should be having. What is it about big data as an aspiration, as a socio-technical category, as a point on the map of our cultural development—what is the work that it is doing for us right now? I could frame the same question in a different way: Why does it feel to me as a woman, as a social scientist who grew up in aboriginal Australia, as a foreigner working in the United States and sitting in those conversations that the truth of big data it is a very particular kind of assertion?

Part of my job—my actual, paid employment!—is to chart the socio-technical imagination. This also entails asking, "what does it mean to have that imagination?" and "how does it get constituted, how do we critique it, how do we make sense of it, how do we open it up for questioning?" When I look at the things that I tend to work on, fear, anxiety, love, lies, God, they are all in some ways part and parcel of a much larger conversation. It is very clear to me right in this moment that big data is the next one of those things that will appear in the socio-technical firmament that is astonishingly right for the kind of anthropological questions that for me are always the most interesting.

Bastard Algebra

Nick Seaver

"Must kinship be dehumanized by mock-algebra?"

In a 1930 essay titled, simply, "Kinship," Bronisław Malinowski wrote about blood and ink:

> Much ink has flowed on the problem of blood—
> "blood" symbolizing in most human languages, and
> that not only European, the ties of kinship, that is
> the ties derived from procreation. "Blood" almost
> became discolored out of all recognition in the
> process. Yet blood will rebel against any tampering,
> and flow its own way and keep its own colour.

He was concerned with the fluid dynamics of relation:
how the blood of affinity courses around the sluices
and levees of kinship systems and how the ink of theory
saturates the pages of the anthropological literature. By
1930, that literature was "flooded" with formalized

kinship theory—large vocabularies of kin terms, diagrams, formulas, algebras, and geometries—and Malinowski worried that anthropologists, borne along on the flood of ink, were leaving the blood of kinship behind.

Where W.H.R. Rivers had enthused in *Melanesian Society* about a future in which kinship studies would "resemble a work on mathematics in which the results will be expressed by symbols, in some cases even in the form of equations," Malinowski was skeptical. "I must frankly confess," he wrote, "that there is not a single account of kinship in which I do not find myself puzzled by some of this spuriously scientific and stilted mathematization of kinship facts."

Kinship, he suggested, was not a matter of mathematics, but "of flesh and blood, the result of sexual passion and maternal affection, of long intimate daily life, and of a host of personal intimate interests." The "bastard algebra" of formalized kinship theory could not hope to capture the lived details of relatedness, and while blood flowed its own way and kept its own color, the ink of kinship theory was at risk of drying out. To capture the "intimate data of family life," Malinowski argued, the study of kinship required "full-blooded descriptions" that flowed more like the relationships in question.

Here was a paradigmatic statement of ethnographic ideals that has guided many researchers through to the present: the descriptive work of anthropology should hew close to lived experience, and formalisms that abstract these experiences into mathematical rules or representations are suspect. But as Malinowski's argument for full-blooded description eased its way into our disciplinary common sense, his argument against formalism left a loose end. We had a way to talk about flows of blood, but not flows of ink. How were we to understand the family situation of bastard algebra itself?

The ocean

When your research requires sitting through many presentations and reading many more blog posts about big data, you become familiar with the stock images often used to represent it. A tunnel lined with blue 1s and 0s curves so its end is just out of sight. A wave, also made of blue 1s and 0s, crashes over the words "BIG DATA," set in a questionable script typeface. Under cloudy skies, a businessman stands in a rowboat, looking to the horizon on a choppy sea made—of course—of blue 1s and 0s.

In popular and critical discourse about big data, water seems to be everywhere. For stock illustrators, the ocean appears to communicate big data's scale, formlessness, and resource-richness. Perhaps they have tapped into that feeling of limitless, ego-centric potentiality Freud called "oceanic." Blog posts warn about drowning in a tsunami of data. Marketers and managers worry about the flood, while engineers talk about working on the plumbing. In his infamous paean to big data and "the end of theory" in a 2008 issue of *WIRED* magazine, Chris Anderson suggested that the scientific method itself was being rendered obsolete by "the data deluge."

The ocean, as Stefan Helmreich has taught us, has a way of dissolving our ideas about relatedness. Underwater, marine bacteria escape from their lineages and smuggle genes laterally among themselves. The soggy link between genealogy and classification—the tree of life and the order of things—breaks apart in the hands of marine microbial geneticists, while new informatic techniques for sorting and specifying relations among species emerge. In the material-semiotic clutch of water and information technology, relations and our ideas about them are promiscuously reconfigured in a state that Helmreich describes as "hyperactive kinship."

If formalism once signified arid reductionism, big data's oceanic imaginaries appear to have rehydrated it. The "vast gulf" between mathematical analyses and daily life that vexed Malinowski has been filled by a flood of data—credit card transactions, page views, the location of your cell phone, clicks, likes, and shares. The flood sustains new calculations that look less like bastard algebras and more like full-blooded formalisms, closer to the descriptive immersiveness of ethnography than to the reductive genealogy of the family tree. As the collection of data quickens and sprawls, the floodwaters threaten to overtake the life they nominally represent: personalization algorithms produce a milieu for our activity online, shaped by and for the collection of data.

Under this sea, a form of hyperactive kinship is at work. Ideas about relationships—between cause and effect, representation and reality, affinity and similarity—dissolve and take new form among big data's devotees. Our daily lives are marked by new links with mathematical formalisms, and new relations are found and forged between all sorts of concepts and data points: search terms and epidemiological forecasts, listening patterns and musical taste, "culture" and the relative frequencies of words in books. A cottage industry has sprung up on the banks of big data, dedicated to sharing the intuitively counterintuitive correlations that spring forth from its algorithmic machinery.

Correlations, to borrow a phrase from Marilyn Strathern, are always a surprise.

But, in spite of grand claims to the contrary, correlations are not enough. As big data swells, it rocks the boats of critical scholars from across the humanities and social sciences who problematize the too-easy forging of relations and remind us that, although it has taken on the appearance of an objective environment, big data is suffused with interpretation and subjectivity. Not everything makes it into the data set, and things that do are transformed. The businessman in the rowboat is probably looking for "insight," and producing insight is more like making lures than pulling up fish—a matter of intentions and construction, not the retrieving of objective relations from an obliging sea of data. In business, big data is used to attract and convince, to capture and compel rather than to prove. In spite of its vastness, its apparent completeness, its seeming objectivity and synonymy with the real, big data is still representation and not reality—ink (or bits), not blood. As Hrönn Brynjarsdóttir relates in her ethnography of Icelandic fishermen and their data, portage between oceans aqueous and informatic is a lot of work.

Dark sciences

As Malinowski noted in 1930, our theoretical problems, like our kin, are inherited. Humanist and social scientific worries about the algorithmic epistemology of big data descend from a long lineage of critiques of objectivity, formalism, quantification, and automation. Malinowski's argument against bastard algebra is a revealing moment in this family history, where a set of enduring and overlapping epistemic divides is cast in the idiom of kinship: the distinction between *naturwissenschaft* and *geisteswissenschaft*, the quantitative and the qualitative, or, as Clifford Geertz would later contrast, "an experimental science in search of law" and "an interpretative one in search of meaning."

We can spot a family resemblance between Malinowski's "full-blooded description" and Geertz's "thick description": both are calls for renewed attention to the blood and sex of daily life, posed against formalistic alters. Where full-blooded description countered the bastard algebra of kinship, thick description was a humanistic alternative to what Geertz called "an ethnographic algorithm"—the post-war American formalisms of ethnoscience, componential analysis, and cognitive anthropology. These approaches, exemplified by the work of Ward Goodenough and Charles Frake, typically understood culture as a system of taxonomic or behavioral rules to be formally elicited and analyzed (what kinds of plants are there and what are they good for? where should newlyweds live? how should one ask for a drink?). Echoing Malinowski, Geertz argued that these formalisms were "obscured by appeals to dark sciences," mistaking their own methods for the essential stuff of cultural life and pretending "to understand men without knowing them."

These dalliances with the dark sciences were also anthropology's first engagements with computers as research tools. Influenced by the cognitive revolution, which took the distinction between hardware and software as a model for the relationship of mind and brain, post-war American formalists avidly pursued the analytic opportunities offered by electronic computers. They worked on new algorithms for multi-dimensional scaling, which could produce models of a culture's taxonomic "spaces." They designed new techniques for formally eliciting cultural data (sometimes called "white room ethnography"), aimed at producing standardized material for computerized comparison. The Wenner-Gren Foundation hosted a germinal symposium in 1962 on *The Use of Computers in Anthropology*, with topics ranging from the electromagnetic workings of computer memory to statistical analysis to numerical ethnological taxonomy. In his introduction to the conference proceedings, Dell Hymes wrote that the future of computing in anthropology depended on two things: the ability to formalize ethnographic analysis and the building of large, systematic, shared data sets—in short, "big data."

But it was not to be, at least for the anthropologists. "Whatever happened to ethnoscience?," Roger Keesing asked in 1972. Maybe the formalism that once called itself "the new ethnography" collapsed under blistering critiques from figures like Geertz, Hortense Powdermaker, and Gerald Berreman. Maybe its theoretical foundations gave out. Maybe, Keesing jokes, the formalists "bored themselves to death." In any case, the symbolic, interpretive, and reflexive turns soon spun the enthusiasm for formalism out of sociocultural anthropology. Ongoing work with computers was relegated to the disciplinary margins, and a long-proposed "Computing Unit" in the American Anthropological Association never made it out of committee. As computational techniques grew in the other social sciences, the methodological sea change computers heralded for anthropology in the 1960s never came to pass, and the details of post-war American formalism are scarcely considered relevant to contemporary anthropological practice, except perhaps as epistemological bogeymen.

Malinowski's and Geertz's critiques of formal analyses echo in contemporary critiques of big data. Where Malinowski had his kinship algebra and Geertz his ethnoscience, we have "data science," the redundantly named, behaviorism-inflected extraction of "insights" from large sets of interactional data. As a result of a sustained effort to keep formalism out, anthropologists today encounter data science as something utterly foreign to the practice of ethnography—a venture-funded epistemology that encroaches on our disciplinary territory, operationalizing concepts like "culture" in troublesome ways. We may recognize relatives of data science in nearby disciplines like cognitive psychology, statistics, and quantitative sociology, but from anthropology and ethnography in particular, it seems to be qualitatively distinct.

Given the history recounted so far, it should not be surprising that ethnography and big data appear as neatly opposed methodological moieties: as long as we have been defining ethnography's richness, full-bloodedness or thickness, we have done it in the negative image of formalism. Our disciplinary understanding of ethnography's strengths is entwined with our understanding of formalism's weaknesses. But where Malinowski and Geertz had few kind words for their formalist counterparts, it is now increasingly common to hear that ethnography is not a competitor with big data, but rather a potential collaborator: In a series of posts on the blog *Ethnography Matters*, for example, neologisms like "thick data" and "long data" (big data's phallogocentric pull is apparently irresistible) offer ways to conceptualize ethnographic research as complementary to big data. Especially in the corporate context, ethnography is tasked with putting flesh on big data's bones, with choosing hypotheses to test, or with validating statistical findings, drawing on standard practices from mixed methods research.

These relationships between methods are, by now, such disciplinary common sense that we might be surprised how much work goes into rehearsing and reinforcing them. Either ethnography and formal analysis compete for jurisdiction over concepts like "culture," or they enter into scripted collaborations with each other, drawing on their apparently complementary strengths. Often, these arguments about how big data and ethnography might get along rehearse claims that have defined ethnography and its relationship to other methods throughout ethnography's entire history. The appearance today that ethnography and big data are meeting for the first time, coming from distinct lineages, has been hard won.

Rather than expending our efforts defending thickness, attacking formalism, or regulating the connections between the two, we might investigate these systems of relating themselves. To put an anthropological spin on it, we could study the kinship of method: How are methodological relationships deemed legitimate or illegitimate? What has the rise of "big data" as a discursive and technical phenomenon meant for the ways methods relate? How do various groups of people—data scientists, ethnographers, managers, advertisers, "users"—themselves partially constituted through these relations, imagine them to work? To talk about the kinship of knowledge, we'll want to draw on our knowledge of kinship.

The kinship of method

"In the same breath," Marilyn Strathern reminds us in *Kinship, Law, and the Unexpected*, "English-speakers find it possible to talk about practices to do with making kinship and practices to do with making knowledge." Words like "conception" and "relation" have long tied together the mental and the parental, and in anthropology, a field originally defined through its interest in kinship, this tendency is only heightened. Strathern outlines how ideas about parentage, causality, ownership, and creation have been shuttled back and forth between Euro-American discourses about family (for example, defining the "mental" conception of a child in surrogate pregnancy) and knowledge (for example, deciding the "paternity" of a bit of intellectual property). This is no idle metaphor. As Strathern notes, "much of culture is a fabrication of resemblances, a making sense through indicative continuities": in the Euro-American context that spawned anthropology, ethnography, and big data, we grasp the facts of kinship and the facts of knowledge with the same conceptual tools. This coincidence offers some promising routes of inquiry for making sense of methodological relations in the time of big data.

To elaborate, let's return to Malinowski's term "bastard algebra." In what sense are formal analyses of kinship "bastards"? Malinowski seems to be suggesting that these methods are the illegitimate offspring of two families of inquiry—the mathematical and the anthropological. Mathematicians would not claim this algebra as their own, and "the average anthropologist," as Malinowski writes, would not either. To this day, many of us remain uneasy about this mixture, and to borrow another bit of kinship terminology, we tend to establish avoidance relationships with mathematics, when we are not dismissing it outright. Like anyone else, anthropologists are concerned with regulating our kinsmen.

But this raises some questions: How do we decide that an algebra is illegitimate, a bastard? Malinowski's answer—that it is not "full-blooded"—should make us uncomfortable both for its resonance with the language of scientific racism and for how it lays bare the weakness of ethnographic authority. How do we know that a description is full-blooded (or "thick")? Are such descriptions a distinctive type, or do we find continuous variation between the bastard and the full-blooded, the thick and the thin?

Early studies of kinship emphasized the role that kin systems played in providing an overriding coherence to social life, especially among "primitive" people, but as we've learned from kinship studies since, bastards and other exceptions to the rules are often so prevalent that they draw into question the idea that strict rules govern at all. In *Pul Eliya*, for example, Edmund Leach drew on ethnographic data (and statistical analysis) to argue that the idea of kinship as a set of overriding jural rules falls apart in the face of actual kin practices, which are much more tied to factors like resource availability and the accidents of personal life. The normative, he claimed, is secondary to the normal.

For our kinship of methods, this turn suggests that we set aside the idea that methodological clans are maintained by their intrinsic coherence. Instead of bemoaning the illegitimacy of bastard analysis and trying to purify our bloodlines, we might take our lead from later work in kinship studies and turn our attention to the lived details of methodological relations: the flows of researchers and research money, legitimacy exchanges, and the *imagination* of normative rules of method that only find partial realization in the spread of actual practices.

The "new kinship studies," especially studies of queer kinship and kinship with new reproductive technologies, are suggestive here, drawing together the study of kin practices that are novel and contested with the reflexive study of "kinship" itself as a category. Relatedness, these studies show us, is torqued by technological change, reconceived through concepts like hybridity and networks, and more unstable than the makers of algorithmic co-relations might want to admit. In his introduction to *The Use of Computers in Anthropology*, Dell Hymes wrote that computers introduced "novel relationships, physical, mental, and social" to anthropology. If we want to understand these relationships, we'll have to suspend our investment in idealized methodological clans and instead seek out the local details of how relations among methods are made, unmade, and regulated.

The shore

Imagine yourself suddenly set down on a beach, waves of blue 1s and 0s crashing behind you. Inspired by fanciful images of big data, you had thought the action was under the sea, but here on the shore, spitting sand, you can see the work it takes to get insights out of the ocean. While big data splashes through popular discourse with its oceanic imagery, disruptively washing away old industries, the talk among these folks is focused on the mundane details of making relations among data points and methods: they want to recommend music based on internet chatter about artists, but the computer has to learn that Justin Bieber and JU$TINNN B3IB3R are the same person; they pipe in metadata from two different companies, but their schemas don't match; somewhere on a server farm, a virtual machine has crashed. This is the real world of data science, and it is simultaneously more boring and more interesting than hype about the world-changing power of data would have us believe.

Here on the shore, we can take what sociologist Celia Lury calls the "frog's-eye view": an amphibious perspective that moves between the watery worlds of big data discourse and the pragmatics of technology in the making. A job posting, for instance, advertises a spot on one of Silicon Valley's many "data teams":

> If you had been born in 800BC you would have been a mystic. You find patterns that others don't see. Maybe you solve disentanglement puzzles in a higher dimensional space without even knowing how you do it.

HR is looking for one of those "new priests and alchemists" Genevieve Bell tells us about, but nobody believes in magic anymore. Or, to put it more anthropologically, nobody realized what belief in magic meant, and as they go about their jobs, they rely on software and studies whose workings they don't fully understand but which they trust to be efficacious. From the history of anthropology and the offhand comments of computer programmers, we know that the boundary between magic and technology is hard to define.

The priests and alchemists may seem like loners, pursuing mathematical truths, but as the Marxist mathematician Dirk Jan Struik reminds us:

"Man is a social being even when he worries about the straight lines on hypercones in seven dimensional space," and our mystics only work through their relations with countless others: maintainers of software infrastructure, lawyers, office managers, quality assurance testers, and interns. These characters all have different theories and concerns about what is going on: the marketing intern is enthusiastic about the idea that big data means "the end of theory." The head of the data team tweets, "No data scientist I know believes tripe like that." The old-guard VP thinks the glut of 20-something machine learning enthusiasts are upstart "hipsters," while the office manager calls them "medium T-shirts," after their common torso size. In meetings, they argue and speculate on how to proceed.

With Pierre Lemonnier's *Technological Choices* and Kath Weston's *Families We Choose* under our arm, we might note that the anthropology of technology and the study of kinships both queer and technologically aided have something in common: they share a concern with choice, flexibility, and legitimate variety in domains where such qualities are often thought to not exist. With our attention cued in this way, we can see how data scientists work as professional bastard-makers, combining data sets, algorithms, and epistemologies in unauthorized ways to produce illicit offspring. This is not the underwater free-for-all of "hyperactive kinship," where it seems like anything might be related to anything else, given enough data, but something more like a tidepool ecosystem, where data, technology, and relationships do not go any which way, but pool and flow along the shore, shaping it in turn. Rather than marvel at the ocean, anthropologists might take to the fractal work of mapping the shoreline.

Bastard ethnography

The imperative to get off the boat and venture ashore is, of course, classically ethnographic in a Malinowskian sense. Spending time among the bastard algebraists of big data is an excellent way to break down our preconceptions about them. From the shore, we can see the variety of people, epistemologies, and methods that constitute "data science." We can see the countless choices involved in cobbling big data together, moments of ambivalence and constraint, and the thickness of formalism in practice.

As big data's oceanic imaginaries dissolve our common sense about relatedness, it is tempting to imagine that ethnography charts a course back to the "real facts" of relations, as Malinowski called them. If formalist algebras bastardize their sociocultural objects, good old-fashioned ethnography, we suppose, can properly reinstall them in webs of meaning, communities of practice, and social structures. Following the example set by late-twentieth-century laboratory ethnography, this would bring both big data and its objects back under our jurisdiction, as practices that are themselves sociocultural and thus best suited to full-blooded description.

But as I have traced here, the relationship between ethnography and its formalist others is not so clear cut, and our understanding of ethnography's strengths is already predicated on formalism's weaknesses. Instead of taking the encounter with big data as an occasion to rehearse this commonsense relationship between methods, we might take it as an opportunity to examine how methods relate. This investigation would not only give texture and specificity to the practices of big data; it would also draw into question ideas about the coherence and self-evidence of anthropology and ethnography.

Kath Weston has described her encounters with the nostalgic idealism of "real anthropology"—a term wielded by those who long for a simple (and non-existent) past, when the work of anthropology was straightforward and clear, untroubled by native anthropologists, queer and postcolonial research, and the breakdown of distinctions between Self and Other. Like other nostalgias, this one is ironically forgetful, failing to recall disputes of the past and the shifting boundaries of what has counted as "real anthropology" over time. Such nostalgias forget, for example, the assumption by many formalists that Geertz's interpretive anthropology would be a passing fad, and they leave us unable to recognize the ways that formal methods banished to the past persist into the present. Weston notes the persistence of Euclidean and Newtonian concepts in avant-garde social science metaphor: "borders, lines, intersections, levels, scales, points, grids, and of course the 'trans' that introduces transverse and transept as well as transnational." Alberto Corsín Jiménez has critiqued social anthropology's "algebraic imagination," through which ideas about relations and how to study them are inflected by mathematical formalisms we had thought were long gone.

The persistence of such ideas—the latent algebra in ethnographic theory, the sub rosa geometries of post-structuralism, the defining interdependency of concepts like "thickness" and "algorithms"—reminds us that ethnography is a bastard too, breeding descriptions from illicit encounters, mixing conceptual schemes, and stirring the blood of experience with the ink of theory. As we examine the family situation of bastard algebra, we will have to come to terms with the bastard status of ethnography itself, remaining open to the ubiquity and generative potential of epistemologies that overflow their borders and relate without permission.

Thanks to Taylor Nelms for his help charting the course of this argument.

The Gift That Is Not Given

Melissa Gregg

Mine eyes are made the fools o' th' other senses,
Or else worth all the rest.

Macbeth

What is it about the current moment that urges so
many to invest in the promise of "big data?" What is it
about big data that makes it so compelling? Is it just
another ripple in the ongoing flow of socio-technical
utopianism? Or does the scale of data as currently
perceived fundamentally change our notion of computing for good? Since its inception, the internet and its
accompanying industries have thrived on moments of
frenzy as the transformative experience of computing is
realized. Ubicomp visionaries set the parameters for
today's exponents of an internet of things, just as social
media evangelists leveraged the desire for connectivity
towards a profitable model of friendship. With data,
however, the sublime capacity of technology is front
and center of the conversation, leaving little need for
web prophets. The magnitude of processing constitut-
ing big data's big-ness invokes technology as a superior
force, allowing vision to be enhanced through the

sheer metrics of aggregation. Technology becomes
God-like: an omniscient and omnipotent presence that
is needed to protect us from what we mortals cannot
know.

Perhaps the first question we need to ask to
begin, then, is "What is big?" before we begin to
answer "What is data?"

What is big?

The comfort to be found in today's techno-empiricism
comes from the achievement of representing data at
scale. In the tech industry, we regularly see the power
of processing celebrated at the expense of considering
the materiality of that which is processed. A company
showcase in San Francisco in 2013 provides a case in
point. At a demo chosen to illustrate the work of a
research center dedicated to "big data," onlookers
were encouraged to watch, electrified, as synchronized
TV screens displayed dynamic images and patterns
panning out from a point of origin. The effect of this
performance was doubtlessly impressive, even if, to a
lay viewer, the morphing blobs of color brought to
mind little more than the lava lamps and fashions of
1970s disco. Engaging the spectator's vision, simulat-
ing the experience of traversing (if not quite "trip-
ping") through data, the demo served the purpose of
illustrating the vastness of the information being navi-
gated. Yet when the presenter was asked, "what is the
data set we are seeing?" it became clear that the data
itself was fictive. There was no actual sample underwriting the demo; *it was just a demo*. The source of the
data was irrelevant for a genre that only requires the

indication of potential. If the tech industry sometimes requires the suspension of such formalist considerations in the work of future-casting, understanding the difference between generic expectation and real life application is just one demand that the new empiricists could be required to answer.

The present fervor over big data visualization makes it easy to forget that debates about scale have been taking place for centuries. The "expansive view" that Bruno Latour critiques in writing about monadology is informed by the ideas of Gabriel Tarde, and before him, Gottfried Leibniz, whose mathematical modeling questioned neat distinctions between individual and collective phenomena. Invigorating this tradition today, Latour's argument outlining "the fallacy of the zoom" contests the very notion of scale. This argument was prominent in his keynote address for the 2013 Association of Computing Machinery's Special Interest group in Computer-Human Interaction (aka "CHI") conference in Paris. The fallacy of the zoom in Latour's terms is that a collective view provides no more accurate a representation than that of an individual—indeed, the expansive view loses much of the latter's specificity. In making this claim, Latour highlights the role played by tools in assembling vision. (Think of a photograph: the frame inevitably constrains and centers attention through a selection process which only possibly remains traceable in the act of viewing). Latour points to the labor that is left out of the frame, lens or medium through which we view representations of reality. This approach acknowledges the selective nature of that which is "given" in what we think we see. The tool of assembly (the camera, say, or the algorithm) has agency in shaping sight towards certainties of apprehension. This recognition allows a degree of caution in thinking about big data when to do so means becoming unusually enamored with vision. It also suggests the relevance of aesthetics in explaining the role that visual pleasure plays in securing solace, excitement and trust. (The Greeks had a term for this: *scopophilia*.)

The logic we appear to find in the appeal to scale is the result of historical accretion. Anna McCarthy's account of the politics of scale (in *Questions of Method in Cultural Studies* 2006), contends that initial definitions of scale rested in part on the musical sense of capturing a sequence of notes in order. Think of the gradually ascending tone structure of instruments we understand to be producing notes higher as opposed to lower in pitch. Like climbing a ladder, the series or progression implied in the idea of scale is a neat way to conceive relative order. We progress by degrees through positions that are taken to be naturally equidistant. Of the 17th century thinkers McCarthy determines as asserting this basic metaphysical hierarchy, Francis Bacon brought mathematical systematicity to the idea of scale. Central to this is an understanding of scale as proportion, which allows the significance of something to be observed "simply by comparing it to other things, without reference to external standards of judgment." As a mode of reasoning, scale eventually stretched to influence not only practices of mapping geographical territory but nascent ideas of political representation as well. Bearing resemblance to a thing—for example, a constituency—confirmed the ability for something or someone to stand in place of and for others. This was also the time that scale could be seen to take an adjectival form. The consequences of this have proven resilient in the longer history of epistemology. Scale provides, as McCarthy writes, a "mechanism of translation, or mapping, which connects material things and their representations in a precise, repeatable, and empirically known relationship which extends to the process of representation in *thought*." Reason could move from the particular to the universal only as a result of these early articulations, which bestowed an obvious logic to graduating concepts of measure.

In McCarthy's reading, scale "helps stabilize a necessarily murky dichotomy: the relationship between physical observation and mental speculation in inductive reasoning." From spatial representations of hierarchy (epitomized in the ladder) to dominant ideas of proportion (e.g. the map), a critical leap is necessary to join individual phenomena and broader conditions. Constructing the bridge between these two measures, McCarthy writes, "scale regularizes the process of knowledge production by implying that there is a proportional relation between the datum, the definite axiom, and the general axiom."

The point here is that scale took on the function of reason through an induction, which constitutes a rhetorical maneuver. To summon the term scale, McCarthy says, is to mobilize "a thread of action and rhetoric actively connecting thought and thing, observation and speculation." The accomplishment of this link, and the continuum of empirical validity it suggests, is what we see playing out in tech demos today. Presenting data at scale invokes an epistemological claim in the mere act of display. It makes permanent what was once only plausible.

What is data?

This takes us to the second of our opening questions. In previous centuries, according to Daniel Rosenberg's "Data Before the Fact" (in *"Raw Data" is an Oxymoron*, 2013), a "datum" was understood as something given in an argument, something taken for granted. The obviousness of data, its *taken-for-granted-ness*, emanated from the Latin origin of the word, which in the singular means "gift," or something that is "given." In the domain of philosophy, religion and mathematics, the term *data* was used throughout the seventeenth century to identify that category of facts and principles that were, by agreement, beyond debate. It referred to things that were assumed, essential to and hence already known before a problem was introduced for discussion. Data contained the parameters or terms of entry for thought, the first principles upon which later deductions would take place. This vital history indicates that data is not the same thing as fact. Data is something presumed *prior to* discussion; a framework creating the *possibility for* discussion. It therefore already contains judgments and decisions about what counts as a *prior-ity* (both priority and *a priori* share the same Latin root; priorities are taken from that which comes before). A data "set," then, "is already interpreted by the fact that it is a set," according to Travis D. Williams (also in *Raw Data Is An Oxymoron*): "some elements are privileged by inclusion, while others are denied relevance through exclusion." The essence of data's ambivalence is that it holds values that are subject to contestation.

Like McCarthy's etymology of scale, these details draw attention to the cultural specificity of reasoning. Even within the context of the English language, from previous usage we see that facts are ontological, evidence is epistemological and data is rhetorical. A datum may also be a fact, just as a fact may be evidence. But, from its first vernacular formulation, the existence of a datum has been independent of any consideration of corresponding ontological truth (after Rosenberg). In today's industry talk, and the growing number of professional contexts in which big data sets are deployed, data's power lies in the assumption that it is synonymous with fact. It is this belief that justifies the most common sense expressions, from "the facts speak for themselves" to "the data doesn't lie." But what is thought of as "common sense," Gramsci reminds us, is itself the result of hegemonic struggle, of power plays aimed at winning consent. In the tradition of speech act theory arising from J. L. Austin, common sense statements can be regarded as *performatives*. They are utterances that carry a rhetorical charge that actualize meaning through the very process of enunciation. Rhetoric, in turn, is a strategy of persuasion in the classical tradition. It is the art of convincing others the veracity and truth of something in spite of selective emphasis and exposure. So while we might continue to think of data as that which is given, as that which is regarded as bearing truth, we can see that the term's shifting emphasis throughout history ultimately removed consideration of its partiality. Through discursive analysis—of rhetoric, etymology and hegemony—data's omniscience appears less solid. These methods allow us to appreciate that only recently did it become typical "to think of data as the result of an investigation rather than its premise," Rosenberg writes. Data disguises as much as it disregards the messiness and contested nature of everyday life, including many things that cannot be "counted" or categorized in order of importance.

Data's consolation

What secret anxiety or hope is being served by the turn to data in its current definition?

One answer is psychological: as Genevieve Bell indicates, there is something reassuring about facts. At a time when workers and consumers might feel overwhelmed by the amount of information available to them, and about them, data can present information in a satisfying because simpler way. It can make the world seem approachable. But just as we must question what is being seen through aggregation, given the hidden labor involved in its assembly, there are problems in assuming that bigger means better data. The fetishization of scale absolves considerations of infrastructure and thus ownership: who is compiling data, for what purposes? This prompts two further questions about the future properties of data, posed by Bell in her contribution to this pamphlet: will everyone produce data? And will everything produce data?

Will everyone produce data?

If big data is inevitably digital data, there are clear limitations on how representative it can be relative to a population. Take the example of FitBit: a popular wearable technology that quantifies the steps an individual takes to encourage a reflective attitude to exercise. Wearables are part of a wider ecology of DIY healthcare that suits users already sensitive to the question of adequate mobility and exercise in the quest to improve health. Will the same kinds of data deliver happiness and health to all citizens? All consumers? Is the desire to produce data of this kind equally felt?

Thinking more broadly, recent efforts to pool data sources—to facilitate the activity seen in state and corporate sponsored hackathons, for example— depends on the provision of citizens' census details as much as their purchasing habits. The chance to improve city services and utilities is a promising frontier to complement market-facing opportunities for data. Still, the app-ification of civic duties and expectations assumes a willing and connected populace with the time and inclination to donate towards a common good. Reporting freeway potholes on a smartphone is only likely to improve driving conditions for those with existing phone service coverage, a license to drive and the motivation to report. What happens if only a limited amount of people engage in this type of data activism, but are held as representative of majority needs? This is the symbolic violence of scale.

Will everything produce data?

The internet of things activated by data is often explained by appealing to the most ordinary experiences: the fridge that can order your groceries, the car that will drive you around traffic. But does it make sense for everything to be a conduit for or responsive to digital data? Are there some things that should not be subject to digitization? Collective memory has always offered signs for us to read as meaningful data: the red sky at night foretelling the shepherd's delight, the red sky in the morning acting as the shepherd's warning. Kenneth Burke described proverbs as "equipment for living." Do social media platforms operate on the same localized address? How do sensors take account of changes to weather, to climate, to seasons when they are designed from specific regions and locales? Where do cultural differences fit in the design of ubiquitous computing? Subtleties of accent are familiar to anyone trying to use voice-activated software. We assume a lot when we assume data sets will speak seamlessly to each other when humans do not.

What would it mean for a sensor to measure a feeling, like love? Can data take on human characteristics—can it lie, make amends, cheat? If data has the same qualifications, features and failings as the human actors that compile it, its effects can be similar to a personal imposition, request or demand. Software protection plans and the limitations of battery life generate frustration when they obstruct our connection with data. Time-sensitive passwords are like forgetful acquaintances who never quite remember that they met you before.

These analogies, while underscoring the agency of objects in assembling our social life, risk reading data transactions as an occasion for anthropomorphism. The remainder of this chapter offers three examples that avoid the tendency to see data as either a friend or enemy (if anything, data's infinite possibilities might be a classic instance of a "frenemy"). These examples see data not as some powerful, quantified and objectified knowledge that is external to individuals—and therefore increasingly out of their control—but as having and enabling agency.

Data agents

Drawing on cultural studies terminology, what are the "ordinary" and "vernacular" uses of data? What methods allow us to recognize that all of us create, store and use data, as much as corporations? For what we already see in the rise of the hackathon, for instance, is the success with which individuals have fought for, and have been granted at least some rights to, the data they generate (see http://wethedata.org for an example of this movement). This is largely a civic phenomenon for the time being, one that assists the political challenge of governance in times of austerity. Opening datasets to hackers solves a problem of human resourcing as much as infrastructure in US cities with insurmountable budgetary constraints. In commercial settings, we are only starting to find a vocabulary for an emerging economy of transaction in which data can bring new opportunities for exchange, wonder and delight. Critical concern has certainly focused on the consequences of data mining, and the relationships imposed upon us by sentiment analysis. But there is also excitement to be found in the prospect of data forming social relationships on our behalf. The proliferation of recommendation services (as Seaver discusses in this pamphlet) and online dating sites are just two of these convivial applications. With data as our agent, algorithms create new matches, suggestions and relationships when we find ourselves unable to do so with the resources at hand. Data agents allow us to contemplate and revel in the unknown possibilities of strangers (as explored by my Intel colleague Maria Bezaitis), fostering collective social practices that mainstream cultures may not wish to draw to light.

In these instances, data acts rather more like our appendage, our publicist, even our shadow. As we know, agents act behind the scenes. Their work happens to one side of the stage upon which a rewarding and profitable performance takes place. Drawing on a similar theatrical framework, Erving Goffman proposed two regions for social behavior: the front region, on show to a public, and the back region, the site of relaxation and regeneration. Both regions host carefully cultivated performances that respond to cues elicited and interpreted in their respective settings. In the data society, a great deal of social work takes place off-stage, by non-human agents, as a result of processing choices engineered by computers. These programming decisions are made before any witnessing takes place by an audience in response to an actor. In orchestrating the setting for the social encounter, algorithms and platforms become default editors for social messages. In assembling and choreographing the stage for digitally mediated performances, they incorporate the work of key grip and set designer. Whether we as individuals want access to this process, this complex infrastructure of assembly, whether we want some say in its operating principles (which include the preferences of engineers), is to insist on the materiality of an encounter regularly sold to us as immaterial. To want a relationship with data agents is part of a broader project of understanding the worth of what communication scholar Vicky Mayer calls "below the line" labor.

Data sweat

Yet the idea of data agents still presumes a degree of distance between the individual and the information that circulates about that individual. It implies segregation as much as a process: I give my data to someone or something that can use it, hopefully to my advantage. Any number of events suggests the naiveté of this optimistic reading, especially where there is a profit to be made. A more generative and accurate way to think about our relation to data that avoids this gift economy is through the body. It is true, for example, that data may cast a shadow when we place ourselves in the glare of certain platforms or transactions. It offers a rough outline of who we are and the form and function of our digital projection for anyone motivated enough to see. But this kind of analogy suggests we have some say in the interactions we choose to make; that we can predict, like the turning of the sun, the ways in which our data will be rendered visible and available.

The idea of data sweat came to me while speaking at a virus protection company in Taipei, in a discussion of privacy and security. The air-conditioned building hosting my talk had varying effects on the guests in attendance. Listeners sitting in the crowded room each had their own way of dealing with the pre-typhoon heat, from fanning to slouching to wiping damp brows. Locals knew that any attempt to leave the building to walk the streets outside would lead to gross discomfort. This contextual awareness led them to make all kinds of climate-dependent decisions, from choice of footwear (no heels) to transport (train or taxi), or just staying late at the office.

Sweat is a characteristically human trait. It is a vital sign that our bodies are working, even if cultural norms differ as to whether this expression should be public. In some cultures, for some people, sweat can show enlightenment, possession or commitment. It can just as easily suggest fear, anxiety or arousal. Given this, sweat can appear at times when we may not want it—leading to perfumes, deodorants and other innovations of disguise and masquerade. Organic, corporeal phenomena like sweat (but also microbes and genomes, as Lana Swartz reminds me) illustrate the existence of data that is essential and that is about us. This is data that speaks, albeit voicelessly, on our behalf.

Sweat literalizes porosity: it seeps out at times and in contexts that we may wish it didn't. It can be an annoyance or an accomplishment depending on the situation. Sweat leaves a trace of how we pass through the world, and how we are touched by it in return. It is the classic means by which the body signals its capacity to "affect and be affected," to use Spinoza's terms. Understood this way, the labor we engage in as we exercise and exchange our data—especially in our efforts to clean up our image, present a hygienic picture and make ourselves look good—is a kind of sweat equity for the digital economy (as my Intel colleague Ken Anderson and I have discussed, and as Bill Maurer considers in this pamphlet).

Data trash

Thinking about data sweat also leads to the notion of exhaust. This is not to signal exhaustion, since we have seen how data production and management often takes place backstage, without our determined effort. Rather, if data is a trail that we leave in our wake as a result of our encounters with the world and things, then this trail conceivably has some undesirable effects. Within the tech industry, "data exhaust" or "tertiary data" names the value that our presence retains after a unique transaction. It seeks to quantify the multiple applications our identifying shadows suggest beyond the gestures of an initial performance. But exhaust is a term with further connotations, especially when thinking ecologically about the hazards posed to an environment.

The clearest example of the environmental impact of data is the investment in property and electricity now required by server farms that hold the world's seemingly infinite packets of information. If data is the new oil, then data centers are the wells and tankers. The move to "cloud computing" is nothing if not a misnomer in this regard.

Data that appears to be pushed to some higher, opaque place requires huge physical infrastructure on the ground. To ignore these relationships, and the geopolitics they engender, is to perpetuate long-standing asymmetries in the experience of computing (see David Pellow and Lisa Sun-Hee Park, *The Silicon Valley of Dreams: Environmental Injustice, Immigrant Workers, and the High-Tech Global Economy*, 2002).

The further consequences of the data traffic moving between pipes and satellites across the globe include the logistical transfer, freight, assembly and dis-assembly of always imminently redundant hardware. Activists are documenting the human impact of this transport, manufacturing and scavenging ecology, from the labor dormitories attached to Foxconn factories to the coltan mines of the Congo. As wealthy countries ship toxic e-waste back to point of origin for disposal, the pleasures enjoyed through new social networks generate an international chain of service and manual labor.

An awareness of data exhaust invites us to take responsibility for the colonial legacy underwriting Silicon Valley mythology, what Paul Dourish and Scott Mainwaring have called "Ubicomp's colonial impulse." Material effects are always attached to the abstract philosophy of freedom promised through computing. If our ideas of data are to remain wedded to the imaginary of prosthetics (as attached to, once it is taken from us) then the notion of exhaust may yet prove to have mobilizing potential. It can bring an assessment of environmental justice to bear upon the mythologies emanating from California's Mountain View.

On not looking a gift horse in the mouth

In his classic, *The Gift*, Marcel Mauss explains that nothing of value ever really comes for free. The forms of obligation that accompany a gift are social and pressing. They involve calculations of honor, status and reciprocity. To offer a gift is to offer a part of oneself—the object is "never completely separated" from the instigator of the exchange. In a highly mediated economy, in which data is often traded without our knowledge, Mauss's theory takes an interesting twist. If we are never fully aware of the context in which our data is given, the social bond that may have formed lacks guidelines and nuance. The terms of obligation demanded of the giver and receiver remain compromised and unclear.

To date, big data has resembled a gift for tech companies seeking to reinvent themselves from the triumphant years of desktop computing. This chapter has shown several reasons why this gift should not be accepted in haste. Data assembled at scale involves responsibilities that play out on several, interrelated levels:

- *use*: the always partial representation of facts produced in data sets involve an inductive leap to which we should always remain mindful. Data and truth are not synonymous;
- *transaction*: an accurate picture of an individual cannot be easily separated or identified, as in a shadow. We gain insights from data through its partial secretion, hence neither the individual nor a single corporation fully owns "our" data;
- *dependence*: given its differential impact on citizens across the globe, the phenomenal waste attached to the generation of data cannot be overlooked. An ethical perspective to data considers the costs involved in demands for its access, provision, use and disposal.

These three points reinforce how much big data takes for granted, since each level comprises any number of contentions. As such, they are offered in demonstration of a necessarily provisional premise: we cannot take data as given. In saying this, and in addition to the many benefits we are already promised in health, security and other services, it should be clear that the further opportunity that is posed by the "moment" of big data is a critical one. It allows an intensification of analytical precision in both the high-tech industry and science and technology studies. This process of refinement includes, fundamentally, insights from humanities and social science disciplines. The references to genre, rhetoric, aesthetics and etymology throughout this chapter reveal just some of the human biases that inflect our perceptions of truth. The vocabulary of post-structuralism, the philosophy of ethics and claims for accountability cannot be wished away by the leap of faith suggested by data omniscience and what Bell calls its new priests and alchemists. Remaining cautious of the benefits of size and scale, and adding vibrancy to the concept of data, we will be better equipped to know the difference between a gift and what is given.

Principles of Descent and Alliance for Big Data

Bill Maurer

As people make use of the Internet and mobile computing, doing everything from reading to shopping to monitoring their own or others' vital signs, the human and the computer, working together, generate a wealth of digital information, "big data," traces of physical and digital interaction and activity. That data in turn creates an economy. What kind of economy is it? What are its signal organizing features, its constituent elements? Economic anthropology from Karl Polanyi to Marshall Sahlins opened the conceptual horizons of "the economy," challenging classical and neoclassical claims about the primacy and universality of the market. Ancient states simply did not have markets, but rather state-centered systems of tribute collection and redistribution. So-called simple societies around the world were based on reciprocity—the exchange of "gifts"—through which boundaries between groups were forged and sundered.

The debate in the early 21st century about the data economy wavers between market metaphors and practices, as well as arguments about redistribution and reciprocity. As we can see in this collection, industry professionals have absorbed *The Gift* and have even taken a page from feminist economic geographer J.K. Gibson-Graham (the pen name of Katherine Gibson and Julie Graham). They have read their Marx and Adam Smith, too, bits and pieces, at least. Patent law and business models alike demand that they attend, and quickly, to the sorts of relations their inventions are helping to create through the creation and exchange of big data.

The internet guru turned critic Jaron Lanier has been at the forefront of thinking through the implications of these relations. *Who Owns The Future*, his 2013 manifesto, is a controversial contribution to the conversation about the new economy of data, and is a useful entry point for a discussion of the kinds of persons and properties inhabiting a world of big data. It proceeds from a particular assumption about the relationship between property and human dignity. The notion of property with which Lanier begins allows him to tell an original primitive accumulation story: the Googles and Facebooks of the world—he calls them "Siren Servers"—are enclosing the commons, luring us to our own evisceration while expropriating us of our data.

I like the argument. I really do. There is also a comfortable familiarity to the story he tells. However, it leaves unaddressed the nature of the data we and the Siren Servers produce in digital networks. My data does not exist without the intercession of the Siren Servers, and the Siren Servers crucially depend on their coproduction of data with me. Lanier's liberal and liberationist manifesto about property does not deal with the profound implications of this relation. Nor does it speculate on what kind of relation it might be, or how it might be performatively enacted or reenacted. Anthropology has as long a history of speculation on such relations as it does of rethinking the economy. Kinship theory, differentiating relationships of generation and descent from marriage and alliance, may provide alternative resources for speculating on data economies.

What if, instead of living through a moment of enclosure and primitive accumulation, we were witnesses to a new era of assisted reproduction, the creation of new beings, multiple and varied, through new kinds of relations of descent and alliance? My conceit is that the creation of new economies of data is like the Baby M case, which, in the late 1980s, began to pull at the fibers of Euro-American parentage by dissociating egg mother from birth mother, leading to questions over the status of who conceives, and in what sense, mentally or physically, and who carries to term? Questions of ownership are pushed back; questions of relation come to the fore.

Lanier argues that nanopayments will ensure human dignity in the digital economy. The central proposition of *Who Owns the Future* is that the political economy of social media and networked computing depends on the extraction of free labor from users, which creates a skewing of reward for effort—a star system, in which the few benefit, and benefit enormously, rather than a normal distribution in which people benefit according to their contributions to the collective endeavor we call the economy. One of Lanier's examples is Instagram, the photo sharing service, which sold to Facebook in 2012 for $1 billion dollars. At the time, the company employed only 13 people. Lanier writes:

> Instagram isn't worth a billion dollars just because those thirteen employees are extraordinary. Instead, its value comes from the millions of users who contribute to the network without being paid for it.

Lanier invokes a principle of "digital dignity" to counter this unfair arrangement. In a world of digital dignity, he writes, everyone would receive a small amount of monetary compensation, a "nanopayment," any time their contribution of data "measured from that person's state or behavior" contributes to the generation of value. The nanopayment would be "proportional *both* to the degree of contribution and the resultant value" (his emphasis). In a world of digital dignity, that data would be the commercial property of the person "behind" it: Lanier uses the metaphor of data as a mask, behind which there is a "real person." Making the data the commercial property of that real person makes it more difficult to deny that there is always a person behind the mask, and highlights that human beings make big data, not the other way around.

Commentators have taken him to task for his next assumption—that monetizing personal data will grow the economy, whose digital manifestation depends on the extraction of data for free from its users. A writer for *Forbes* noted that all that providing nanopayments for data would do is increase the measurable economy, the calculation of the GDP, but it wouldn't necessarily actually affect people's ability to consume. Still, as a writer for the *New Republic* put it, Lanier is criticizing the business models of Silicon

Valley which through "dishonest accounting" allow the current state of affairs to continue: unremunerated data collection from millions of users whose activities add to the value of if not outright constitute the "big data" digital economy. There is an economic case for nanopayments—rejected by many commentators—but also a justice case, like the "Wages for Housework" campaigns of the 1970s. Getting the accounting right aligns for Lanier with "dignity." In this assessment, Lanier is very close to Aristotle in *Nichomachean Ethics*, for whom justice was a matter of proportionality, an "equality of ratios," as achieved with money as a medium of exchange, while "the unjust is what violates the proportion. Hence one term becomes too great, the other too small, as indeed happens in practice; for the man who acts unjustly has too much, and the man who is unjustly treated too little, of what is good."

Lanier draws together money, accounting and people, for an accounting as if people mattered. It is not surprising to this anthropologist of money that money itself occupies a central chapter in Lanier's book. There, consistent with the notion of dignity and inner worth of the person, Lanier exhorts his readers to remember that money is a memory device—he does not cite the famous anthropologist, Keith Hart, who made this argument the centerpiece of his oeuvre, nor does he cite the groundbreaking work of archaeologist Denise Schmandt-Besserat, whose discoveries involving artifacts from ancient Mesopotamia helped seal the deal for the origins of money in record-keeping practices (though he mentions the artifacts from which she drew her conclusions). Historically, money was a way to record and remember debts. It was a solution to an accounting problem, not a commodity in itself.

Modern money, however, passing from hand to hand, anonymously, lulls its users into forgetfulness. We become ignorant of the true source of money's value: ourselves. It is a small step, then, from the belief in the gold standard to digital money schemes like Bitcoin (which Lanier does not mention), which partakes of "the fallacious hope that information technology can make promises on its own, without people."

There are historical echoes and analogues of dignity and humanism. This is an unabashedly humanist text, and there's nothing wrong with that from my point of view. Indeed, like David Graeber's *Debt*, which Lanier invokes in the money chapter, Lanier's book is important for popularizing some key ideas in alternative theories of economics, ideas which have been gaining some traction in political, activist and intellectual circles. It also, by drawing attention to the human in the digital economy, spotlights the fact that value is only created through relationships. It is not some free floating, transcendent good, but something actively forged, debated, built by people living together with each other. This is always a useful thing to be reminded of.

Yet the concept of the human in this book is impoverished. It is also Eurocentric. The notion of dignity Lanier advances sounds like it came straight from Thomas Aquinas. The idea of a nanopayment sounds like a "just price" from the Salamanca school who, as Taylor Nelms has pointed out, not coincidentally were debating the status and property of the newly discovered peoples of the Americas.

Now, Lanier may intend these echoes. We are like the serfs of the feudal age whose digital labors are expropriated by our overlords Facebook and Google. Or, we are like the Indians of the New World, our properties stolen from us, our persons soon to be enslaved or annihilated.

As someone who has been making the case for a while that the contemporary economy we call capitalism has a lot of non-capitalist elements central to its operations, I am sympathetic to the argument, and feel gratified any time arguments for the neo-feudal character of the economy make it into the wider public debate. As someone who takes pains to demonstrate the public infrastructures supporting a great deal of private wealth creation, I appreciate Lanier's discussion of the role of the commons and the dangers of creating closed loops that channel economic and social activities into one, privately held set of rails (he contrasts Apple with public rights-of-way).

But Lanier is rehashing an old, old story. A story about human dignity in the face of the enclosure of the commons. A story about the private property that inheres in the human person and the penumbra created by its labor. Lanier is calling for a liberal revolution that would free the digital market from the "levees" currently put in place by the Amazons, Googles and Facebooks that channel the flow of information, money and labor back to themselves. Again, Lanier's term for these companies is Siren Servers, which lead men and presumably women astray with their sweet song promising efficiency, access and speed. Demanding a nanopayment is, in effect, the demand of the creation of another levee that channels value back to users/consumers. Lanier seems to be echoing Karl Polanyi, who argued that when market excesses intrude too far on human freedom and flourishing, "society" must push back, to keep capitalism human. Lanier is a bit ambiguous on whether nanopayments are themselves a new levee or create the conditions of possibility for more gradual, smoother, less concretized ones. It is interesting to me that there is a homological slippage and etymological connection in English between levee—a water-controlling embankment—and levy, a tax or a state appropriation of property in the event of nonpayment of taxes. Both derive from the French *lever*, to raise. The taxation sense of the term is the more ancient, dating to the Renaissance. The water management sense, appropriately enough, dates to the industrial revolution. Neither allows for free flow. Each could be said to be a non-market intervention in an otherwise open economy, or an economy that would be open if not for all of the levees/levies currently channeling and redirecting and reshaping resources, production, value creation and circulation.

But property is a relation. Lanier uses the commonsense notion of property as a thing. The thing in question is data. Sometimes, the thing in question, the data, is a part of us; other times, it is us. (I would note here the We The Data project of Intel Labs, but set this aside for others to comment on.) Jay MacDonald, a reporter with *Credit Card News*, which interestingly enough interviewed Lanier, said his first book, *You Are Not A Gadget*, might as well have been called *You Are Data, And That's Worth Something*. The image is somewhere between that of John Locke's definition of property as a thing with which I have mixed my labor (or, infamously in Locke, labor under my control, such as that of my horse or my slave, taken as extensions of my legal personality), and *The Matrix*, where my very body provides the energy that powers a world of machines.

But property is not a thing. Property, classically understood, is a relation. It is a relation between persons with respect to things. In the case of my

Google profile, the data (I will henceforth just call it "the data" rather than "my data" or "personal data" for reasons that will become clear) is in Lanier's formulation either mine or Google's, the latter having expropriated it from me. Lanier's nanopayment proposal does not expressly oppose alienation. He just wants us to be paid for it. This is the Lockean logic. The value of the data comes from what I have added to it in order to constitute it.

Data, however, needs at least two to tango. Google is not Nature. It has a secret life, after Genevieve Bell; it has a backstory that tells of its origins. If we follow the Lockean paradigm, then the data is something created when I added my labor (my "clicks," my "likes," my shopping choices, my payment information, my location) to something in the commons—to Nature. Locke was trying to figure out how to justify a world of private property in which everything had been given In The Beginning to Adam. The answer was that humanity had dominion over everything. But an individual man could only claim as his property that which he had removed from Nature and altered by adding his labor (or his horse's, or his slave's) to it.

But Google is not Nature. Google is another entity, indeed, a corporate and legal person. So, I have not added my labor to Nature, a global commons, but to a privately created and owned system. (Nature, incidentally, is not nature either, if we have learned anything from Donna Haraway, but a complex of natures-cultures. It is never simply given to "man," nor is "man" ever simply encompassed by it.) That system has considerably less value (in multiple senses of the term) without the data that I contribute to it. But I can't even contribute that data absent that system.

Would it make sense then to see the data as the co-production of myself and Google? Would it make sense to see the network linking me to Google as a site of production? or even, as a site of generation? as a marriage?

The relation Lanier wants is a "full-fledged commercial relationship" between Google and me. He wants me to have "inalienable commercial rights to data that wouldn't exist without" me. But, as I've said, the data also wouldn't exist without Google.

Often when journalists, critics or even anthropologists want to draw a distinction between commercial relationships and other kinds of relationships, they call the other kinds of relationships simply, "relationships." Recently a businessman introducing himself to me indicated that he, like me, had an interest in "culture" because he understood that there were differences between "relational economies" and "task-based economies." One often reads or says or teaches that capitalist relations "flatten relations," the relations presumed to be fuller, more multifarious or complex before subjected to the commodity calculus, the use of money as a universal yardstick for measuring value, or the wage relationship. In an essay for *Hau: The Journal of Ethnographic Theory* titled "Sorting out commodities: How capitalist value is made through gifts," the anthropologist Anna Tsing writes that "[c]apitalist commodities... come into value by using—and obviating—non-capitalist social relations, human and non-human."

Here's how our reasoning often goes. First, we (almost nonsensically) contrast a world of relations to a world of commodification where relations are flattened or obviated. The task then becomes to excavate the relations, to show they're there, to demonstrate their importance—or to mourn their loss. Second, we think relations are good. They are good, good, good. There is always a virtue in the relation. It is about connection, not disconnection; inalienability, not alienation; the full human, not the eviscerated serf or automaton. Third, we then make all kinds of claims about that good, relational world, generally presuming that we know relations when we see them and that what we see is self-evident. But is it?

The datas and their relations to each other and with us and the Googles out there may be far more interesting than the liberal humanist or commercial framework will allow, and may offer other possibilities for imagining a politics.

What Kind of Relation is The Data? In *The Relation*, Marilyn Strathern pointed out that the use of the term "relation" to refer to the "joining of persons" (originally, through marriage or "blood" ties)—the root sense of social relation—emerges in English only in the sixteenth and seventeenth centuries, right around the time of European exploration, conquest and justifications for private property. Before then, relation referred to a narration, the telling of a story. There is, she notes, a "consistent parallel, the repeated echo, between intellectual propagation and procreative acts, between knowledge and kinship" in the slippage between conception as an idea and conception as a procreative process, between relation as a story of logical interconnection and relation as a kinsperson. That slippage became evident and consequential in the Euro-American scene, Strathern argues, when the new reproductive technologies displaced rights in a child from its (biological) conceiver to its (mental or "intentional") conceiver, from, in a celebrated legal case from California in 1993, birth mother to the couple who had contracted her to carry a child to term, who had the initial "mental concept" of the child (the judge's term) and who thus "merit[ed] full credit as conceivers."

Who has the credit for the conception of the data? Another way of posing this question is, what kind of relation is the data? Is it my child, the offspring of Google and me? Is Google the original "conceiver" and am I more like the surrogate mother? Or is it the other way around? Alternately, does conception not matter so much as the alliance, the relation forged between Google and myself through the exchange of gifts, and the resulting products of our co-laboring?

Indeed, there are multiple "datas" here and they interact. (They're not even distinct data sets, really, and I employ the grammatically awkward "datas" to refer to them.) Every time an application updates on my mobile phone, I am told which "data" the application will access. The data is a relation—a kinsperson—and it has other relations with other relations.

Our Data, Our Selves? Or Our Data, Our Children or Siblings?

What Kinds of Relations Can We Have With Our Relations? In Lanier's model of human dignity, the datas would all be taken to be extensions of my single personality. This is, as I have said, a liberal humanist model, and a Eurocentric one. But I still like it, quite a bit—don't get me wrong! Absent other alternatives, I am just fine with joining the argument for the extension of commodity relations into our relations with the datas, and holding out the hope for a more relational economy in a time to come, while continuing, also, to point out that that relational economy is already here, if we care to look for it.

I want to go all anthro on Lanier. I will do so now, fully aware that in doing so, I am committing another kind of relation-trick: that of relativism. But bear with me.

A relativist take on relations would claim: relations always mean different things. What a biological father "means" here, might not be the same as what a biological father "means" there. This is not the kind of relativism *I* mean, however. I remain one of those anthropologists who really does not think it is possible to write other worlds in this world—my world, the English language, the words on the page written in a particular sequence and with a particular grammatical structure and frames of reference and pragmatic cues on how to read, embodied in the very materiality of the electronic screen or physical page itself. I think the only solution to this is to try to create, or to discover, others' projects (for want of a better word), others' ways of doing and knowing that are taking place alongside our own, and to see if we can follow beside them for a while. We won't pretend to approximate, or to replicate. But we might see if along the way there are resonances we can hear that suggest other possible worlds. (Dear reader, we can take this up at another time.)

Let me postulate that relations not only have different meanings, then. They also are produced in different *practices*, practices that unfold in different *temporalities* of action, and in terms of different styles or idioms.

This is the approach taken by anthropologist Jane Collier in her analysis of marriage and inequality in non-capitalist societies. Collier did for alliance what Strathern did for descent, consanguinity and procreation. Collier began with marriage because marriage is where relations are made and sundered and around which gifts and payments circulate. She posed three distinct models for understanding relations based on the kinds of exchanges that take place around marriage in classless societies supposedly characterized by "the gift" (thus considerably complicating what we mean by "gift"). What she discovered in the process was that things like gifts and debts, far from securing or sundering one kind of relationship, involved very different practices, temporalities and styles. I will provide just two examples. It is impossible to do them justice, but I intend for them just to get the creative juices flowing on other ways of thinking about relations. These are indeed the bloodless algebras Nick Seaver recalls in his contribution to this volume. I want to see if we can grow new meat on their bones.

In what Collier calls the Equal Bridewealth Model, exchange relationships are demonstrations of one's claims to others, which are figured through an idiom of "respect." Elders organize work, but everyone has access to the tools they need to make a living for themselves. To get married, however, you need to give gifts, and to get the gifts to give, you need help from elders. Those gifts belong to the elders, and their quality and quantity indicate their perception of the worthiness of the groom. But the gifts actually derive from the work of the elders' dependents. Elders want to accumulate a lot of dependents. One has to demonstrate respect to get respect. One does not work to get things, but to get respect, which will translate into gifts from elders to give to wives' kin. Mother/son relationships here matter because a son can appeal to a mother for assistance in assembling goods needed from elder men for gifts and, if an elder refuses, the mother can redeploy the efforts of her children away from her husband, thus denying him a route to respect. Women are thus often seen as both the giving mother and the disruptor of social harmony.

In what Collier calls the Unequal Bridewealth Model, relationships and exchanges are demonstrations of rank. People are presumed to be born into unequal ranked statuses. Yet rank can fluctuate and is unstable, so it has to be constantly demonstrated. Marriages are key occasions for validating rank. Wife-givers outrank wife-takers, that is, a husband is always "downhill" from a wife's brother, but marriage is an opportunity to climb rank by paying more for a high-ranking bride. How to accumulate what you need to make that payment? Your siblings, if subordinate to you, can provide you with the things you need to assemble a good payment. So, the sibling set is very important but also a site of constant jockeying for position. By exten-sion, different sibling sets are themselves always jock-eying for position in negotiating marriages so that one can climb rank. If you exchange nearly equal gifts, things can remain relatively stable, but as soon as some-one falls behind, he might need to borrow, pushing him even further behind. Gift exchanges are arenas for displaying rank. Sibling relationships here matter because they provide access to resources needed to affirm the entire sibling set's rank relative to other sibling sets. Gender and generation fade; rank is primary.

These thumbnails hardly do justice to Collier's models or to the ethnographic and historical material, much less the people behind the stories. And she devised other models, besides these two. Let's spin out a few implications from them. Let's take Bell's anthro-pomorphisms to a new anthropological level. And, again, let's imagine that we are standing in relation to "big data" where people were in relation to the New Reproductive Technologies at the time of the Baby M case.

Are we making children with Mother or Father Google? When I am the co-creator with Google of the data, is that data our child? What kind of claim do we have over that child, and what kind of claim do others have?

It all depends on who are the "conceivers" here, but if we start from the assumption—which we can challenge later—that Google and I are the co-creators, then what? That child wants to go out into the world. To do so, it needs to assemble a gift to permit it to co-mingle with other data. That gift has to be a demonstration of its respect for that other data's co-creators (say, you and Google, or you and Amazon). How is it going to do that? Google and I have to determine how worthy we deem that child, and it has to demonstrate its respect for us in order for us to make that determination. Things can change over time, and circumstances matter. (One might invoke the philosopher Helen Nissenbaum here, for whom context in data relations is everything.) But our decision to allocate the stuff it needs to co-mingle with other data depends on its giving us its labor as a sign of respect, and as an augmentation of our own capital. It has to work for us. Its and our gifts thus fulfill obligations and earn respect (I am tracking Collier pretty closely here).

One could spin this out further depending on whether it is Google or myself in the position of mother or father. *Nota bene* that mother and father here are social roles based on gift relationships with others, not biological "relations."

Are we the siblings of the datas, and who is jockeying for rank with whom? When lots of datas get created with lots of other entities (Google, Facebook, Amazon, etc.) are we all siblings? What kind of claims do we have on each other and what kinds of exchanges help us assert or change our rank?

A lot depends on how we determine who outranks whom. In Collier's Unequal Bridewealth Model, marriage is where such contests over rank take place. An easy way out is to either start with me (the embodied me) as outranking all the datas, or with the corporate persons (Google, Facebook) as outranking everyone else, or as me and the corporate persons together outranking our siblings, etc. But we can certainly start to model just by tracking apps' use of the datas, how the datas enact rank relationships with each other and the effort to raise one's position in a ranked hierarchy through things like the pushing of a platform during an app update ("upgrade now and click here to import all your contacts to Google+"). The terms themselves suggest the ordinality of rank relations: *up*date, *up*grade.

When *Johnson v. Calvert* was decided in favor of the "intentional" parents in 1993, a debate was launched over the status of the supposed biological facts of reproduction. Marilyn Strathern pointed out that the idea that a mental conception took precedence over a biological one, while alien at the time for Euro-Americans, is precisely how some Melanesians think about the person—as always an idea first before being a substantial being. Today, with Lanier's Siren Servers and "my" personal data, we are having a debate over payment and ownership. But what kind of labors generate that data? Ought we to think in terms of alliance and generation rather than wages and work?

If nothing else, doing so would provide more conceptual tools for understanding where we stand with regard to the datas and the Googles and Facebooks. Instead of assuming we're in the middle of a kind of primitive accumulation based on big data, we might consider whether we are negotiating a new kind of marriage. To dignity, one could counterpose respect, or alternately rank. These would each have different implications for unpacking current systems, and imagining new ones. I do not mean to sound too Pollyannaish, but I also don't see how we can think about "our" data without acknowledging the fact that it doesn't exist outside "the relation."

My point is to see if the empirical reality of us and the datas and the Googles might demand some deeper thinking than dignity. Until that time, I would be pleased to accept a nanopayment.

Making Big Data, In Theory

Tom Boellstorff

Introduction

We live in a time when big data will transform society. Or so the hype goes.

Like any myth, the current hullabaloo regarding big data is overblown but contains grains of truth. There are the relatively easy responses: there is no unitary phenomenon "big data." There is no singular form of "society." And so on. Yet the impact of big data is real and worthy of sustained attention.

You may have noted that I am not capitalizing "big data." This is my first theoretical intervention building on, as Genevieve Bell noted in the first piece in this pamphlet, the question "How do we start talking about the socio-technical imagination?" My goal is to explore four ways to start talking about the socio-technical imagination, and in so doing to forge the "big theory" sorely needed in regard to big data. I ground these explorations in my primary disciplinary background of anthropology but draw from other fields: etymology as much as ethnography, philosophy as much as science studies.

This essay originates in conceptual interests that have haunted me throughout my work on digital culture and also my earlier research on sexuality in Indonesia. There is also a proximate motivation: the Edward Snowden affair of 2013. His disclosure that the National Security Agency was monitoring domestic "metadata" launched a vociferous debate about big data, surveillance and the public good. At various points I will draw on aspects of the Snowden affair and the broader discussions linked to it, particularly as they connect to our interest in "speculative civics" and the ongoing value of the "public" in an age of data.

This chapter covers a great deal of conceptual ground: I am less interested in offering closure than opening conversations. Concepts I will develop include "dated theory," "metastasizing data," "the dialectic of surveillance and recognition," and "rotted data." The title "Making big data, in theory" flags the themes of "making" and "theory" that appear throughout. There is a great need for theorization precisely when emerging configurations of data might seem to make concepts superfluous—to underscore that there is no Archimedean point of pure data outside conceptual worlds. Data always has theoretical enframings that are its condition of making.

The stakes are high. Algorithmic living is displacing artificial intelligence as the modality by which computing is seen to shape society: a paradigm of semantics, of understanding, is becoming a paradigm of pragmatics, of search. Contemporary computational language translation, for instance, does not work by trying to get a computer to intelligently understand language: systems like Google Translate work by matching texts from a vast corpus, without the computer ever "knowing" what is said. Historically this lack of knowing was a problem to debate, as in "Chinese room" thought experiments questioning if a person locked in a room and given English instructions for using Chinese characters could be said to understand Chinese. But while the possibility of artificial intelligence is certainly still debated, what is most striking is the degree to which such questions have simply been set aside. Moreover, emergent paradigms of algorithmic living pose the possibility that pragmatics and semantics might converge, that "use" will be the "meaning" that matters in what is claimed to be a new age of big data.

Big data—this vast and changing corpus—is thus at the heart of the idea that a shift to algorithmic living is nigh, despite the concept's relative novelty. The term "big data" likely dates informally to the 1990s, first appearing in an academic publication in 2003 but gaining wider legitimacy only around 2008. Nonetheless, in less than a decade big data rose to a dominant position in many quarters of the technology sector, academia and beyond. Massive amounts of grant money, private- and public-sector labor and capital—corporate, state and military—now flow into the generation, capture and analysis of big data. The humanities and social sciences face threats and opportunities, not least because "ethnography" is often presented as the Other to big data, raising fascinating issues regarding their recombination. It is vital that a vibrant theoretical discussion shape these emerging paradigms, for "big data" is poised to play an important role regarding the mutual constitution of technology and society in the twenty-first century.

Dated theory

Spatial metaphors of mobility and omnipresence are salient in discussions of big data, but big data is also a profoundly temporal phenomenon—caught up in debates over time, technology and theory. Consider how I speak of the Snowden affair, even though by the time this chapter is published those events will have changed. What does it mean to say that by the time you read this chapter it will be dated? Have I thereby limited its utility: will it be interesting in 2016, in 2026? Could there be any relevance to being behind?

I want to pause on this issue of the timely, an issue that seems ever to nip at the heels of discussions regarding big data and the digital more generally, threatening analytical purchase. I want to consider the value of arguments whose time is out of joint, that are dated. Developing what I will term "dated theory" is important for addressing relationships between big data, representation, surveillance and recognition.

My notion of "dated theory" is informed by the history of the data concept. In his article "Data before the fact," which appeared in Lisa Gitelman's edited volume *"Raw Data" Is an Oxymoron*, published in 2013, Daniel Rosenberg traced its rise in the seventeenth and eighteenth centuries. He noted it "is the plural of the Latin word *datum*, which itself is the neuter past participle of the verb *dare*, to give. A 'datum' in English, then, is something given in an argument, something taken for granted." But my linking "data" to "dated" does not invoke a false cognate. As the *Oxford English Dictionary* reminds us, "date" also comes from *datum*, a shared etymology that is a literal effect of "correspondence," given that it originates in a phrase used when referring to the time a letter was sent. "Data," then, has long been connected to the time of a letter's sending—what is now termed "metadata," a central topic of the Snowden affair. By "dated theory," I mean to foreground how data is always a temporal formation; "data" always has a "date" that shapes claims to truth made on its behalf.

The notion of dated theory is useful due to fears that our own research is in constant danger of obsolescence. One thing that clearly contributes to such unease is the idea that analytical value hinges on anticipation. This is shaped by positivist traditions that equate scientific value with predictive laws, as well as the hype-filled rhetoric of Silicon Valley showmanship, where "trending" is at a premium. As Paul Dourish and Genevieve Bell note in their book *Divining a Digital Future*, this rhetoric also shapes scholarship: "the dominant tense... is that of the proximate future. That is, motivations and frames... portray a proximate future, one just around the corner." This recalls prolepsis, the literary device of the "flashforward" that appears in a phrase like "you're a dead man" when spoken by a villain to the person about to be murdered.

To respond to the proleptic temporal imaginaries that often accompany big data, it can be helpful to recall that knowledge production is never separate from the knowledge producer. A discussion of dated theory is a discussion of dated theorists. Consider the well-documented temporal politics of anthropology. Johann Fabian has noted how a legacy of anthropology's origins in colonialism was a tendency to portray those being described as in an earlier time. Within anthropology, this tendency has been deeply critiqued, and this has in turn shaped a critique of the dominant temporal imaginary of its practitioners. This is the trope, perhaps best known through the mythical image of the pioneering Bronisław Malinowski, where a lone anthropologist arrives at a tropical island and "discovers" a "remote" tribe whose members have ostensibly lived unchanged for centuries.

In contrast, there has been little discussion of the temporal imaginary of big data researchers. How does time shape their subjectivities and the making of big data? It may be that the temporal imaginary is not one of digging into the past but looking into a future more than proximate—a *distal future* that can be predicted and even proleptically anticipated.

And the paradigmatic figure of this researcher? One candidate might be Hari Seldon, the protagonist of Isaac Asimov's classic 1951 science fiction novel *Foundation*. Seldon, the greatest of all "psychohistorians," has been put on trial by the Galactic Empire, twenty thousand years from now. His crime is one of anticipation: to threaten panic by using what we can term big data to predict the Empire's fall. Seldon's defense is that he seeks to create an "Encyclopedia Galactica" to save all knowledge and thereby shorten the subsequent period of anarchy.

Asimov's Wikipedia-before-its-time, his vision of what we can anachronistically but accurately term "big data as social engineering," resonates with a contemporary context where the purpose of data is increasingly seen to lie in the future, be that one's health at retirement or a traffic jam down the road. Now, I am not claiming that all those who work with big data have read Asimov or aspire to be Hari Seldon, any more than all ethnographers wish to discover an "untouched" native tribe. My point is that we need to "date" not just big data but the temporal imaginaries shaping those who use it.

Making metadata

The Snowden affair foregrounded an ostensible subset of big data, "metadata"—taken to mean things like the time a cellphone call was placed, its duration and the caller's location, in contrast to the conversation itself. A fundamental power move by representatives of the United States government was to contend that NSA surveillance practices were benign because at issue was only metadata. Attempts to depoliticize metadata thus hinged on asserting a self-evident distinction between data and metadata, and critical responses often challenged this claim. This shows how one of the most pressing issues in regard to theorizing big data involves historicizing metadata and mapping out its conceptual implications.

The notion of metadata precedes that of big data, having been coined in 1968 by the computer scientist Philip R. Bagley (1927–2011). In using the *meta-* prefix at the dawn of the Internet age, Bagley drew on layers of history with embedded assumptions. In particular, the prefix contains an *unacknowledged tension between laterality and hierarchy*. This tension has never been resolved, with implications for power, selfhood and community.

Prior to Bagley's coinage, in the study of language, information and communication *meta-* dates to the 1950s, when the linguist Roman Jakobson began developing the notion of "metalanguage" to refer to language about language—for instance, "I dreamed of a unicorn" is language, and "a unicorn is an imaginary horse with a single horn on its head" is metalanguage.

Jakobson referred to the mathematician Alfred Tarski in writing about metalanguage, and in doing so revealed a second history of the meta- prefix, linked to "metamathematics"—a term developed by David Hilbert in the 1920s, but connecting to scholarship going back to thinkers like Russell, Frege, Gödel and Whitehead. It is this tradition that seems to have most directly influenced communication studies and thus big data. For instance, the authors of the foundational 1967 text *Pragmatics of Human Communication* introduced their theory of "metacommunication" by analogizing it to the notion of metamathematics.

Throughout the twentieth century use of the *meta-* prefix expanded, including metaknowledge, metaindexicality, even metaculture. Yet the prefix has retained a fundamental instability. On one hand it is used hierarchically: this is the framework of a zero-degree referent (e.g., language, knowledge or data), and then "meta" phenomena that lie above or below. On the other hand (sometimes by the same author) the *meta-* prefix is used laterally—so that, for instance, metalanguage is language about language itself.

The origin of this double sense of the meta-prefix is rarely addressed: "meta" is not yet a well-dated theory. Consider μετα's long history, in which the prefix originally had only a lateral meaning: as the *Oxford English Dictionary* reminds us once again: "[I]n ancient Greek and Hellenistic Greek the prefix is [used] to express notions of sharing, action in common, pursuit, quest, and, above all, change (of place, order, condition, or nature)." This original meaning lies at the heart of mass and digital "media": the German media theorist Friedrich Kittler one noted that Aristotle linked the original meaning of *metaxú* as "between" to the philo-sophical concept *tò metaxú* (medium). "Metamedia" is a redundant term given this original meaning of the *meta-* prefix. This laterality is now nearly forgotten, appearing in only a handful of terms. These include "metaphor" (literally, "to carry across"), "metathesis"—and, most interestingly, "metastasis," which as Bill Maurer noted in his article "Creolization redux" had by the late Renaissance become a medical term regarding the transference of function between organs. Metastasis effected a change of state, not a state above; there may be value in theorizing data that "metastasizes."

But if μετα originally referenced laterality— "before" and "after"—how did it come to take on the hierarchical, abstracting meaning contained in phrases like "going meta?" It was classification error, a mistake in book shelving. The scholar Georgios Anagnostopoulos noted in *A Companion to Aristotle* that Andronicus of Rhodes, who in the first century BC created what became the definitive edition of Aristotle's works, bound several of Aristotle's writings together and placed the volume after (*meta-*) Aristotle's works on physics. "Metaphysics" thus literally referred to the books "next to" the Physics, and at that point μετα had no sense of transcendence. Only in subsequent centuries did the notion of metaphyics (and the *meta-* prefix more generally) come to imply an overarching or higher state.

This history of misinterpretation is hardly obscure; it can be found on the "meta" entry on Wikipedia. In recounting it I mean to imply neither etymological determinism nor Eurocentrism. At issue is rather the deafening silence regarding the term's contingency and the tensions built into the *meta-* prefix itself. Specifically, *the notion of "metadata" is derived from this mistranslation of "metaphysics"* away from laterality and toward hierarchy. Particularly from the seventeenth century, "metaphysics" took on a strongly Christian cast: it may be that the only novel use of *meta-* as a prefix prior to the nineteenth century comes from John Donne's 1615 conception of a "meta-theology" above the personal Gods of the Reformation. That metadata might be shaped by these notions of metaphysics is worthy of attention in a domain where some people describe themselves as "technology evangelists" and use "avatars," sometimes on Apple computers whose logo recalls the bite from the Tree at Knowledge in the Garden of Eden (a fact noted as long ago as 1991 in Judith Halberstam's article "Automating Gender").

The pivotal point is that the threshold that causes something to move from a zero-degree category to its "meta" analogue is not a priori, but an act of classification. I seek to challenge assumptions of a neat division between data and metadata not just because metadata can be more intrusive than data, but because the very division of the informational world into two domains—the zero-degree and the meta—establishes systems of implicit control. Indeed, once a zero-degree/meta distinction is accepted, it becomes impossible to know when to stop. For instance, if we assume that to talk about language one must use a "metalanguage," then as far back as 1967 the authors of *Pragmatics of Human Communication* had already noted we need "a metametalanguage if we want to speak about this metalanguage, and so forth in theoretically infinite regress." So data about metadata could be termed "metametadata," but the fact that a "theoretically infinite regress" is built into the *meta-* prefix indicates a flaw with the concept—namely, obviating the contestable social practices by which data is constituted as an object of knowledge.

These issues around metadata are not limited to the online. During the Snowden affair many were surprised to learn of a longstanding system of monitoring physical metadata, the Mail Isolation Control and Tracking program, where the US Postal Service has long been photographing the outside of mail they process. Here, the division between data and metadata might seem beyond debate (as well as recalling the historical link between writing "data" on an envelope and being "dated"). After all, what could be easier to distinguish than the address written on an envelope from the letter inside it?

However, I want to question this and all divisions between the zero-degree and the meta. What if the division was framed not in terms of letters in envelopes with their interiors and exteriors, but the two sides of a postcard? Postcards were controversial during their emergence in the late nineteenth century because their "contents" could be read by anyone; they trouble the distinction between form and content. How might analogizing the postcard provide one way to rethink this binarism? If I could take a postcard and bend it into a Mobius strip I would be even happier: a vision of form and content as intertwined at the most fundamental level, such that acts of "meta" assignation are clearly the cultural and political acts they are, rather than pregiven characteristics.

It is not just that terming things "data" is an act of classification; terming things "metadata" is no less an act of classification and no less caught up in processes of power and control. It is founded in a long and convoluted history of tensions between hierarchical and lateral thinking that shape everything from file systems to societies. This history undermines any attempt to treat the distinction between zero-degree data and metadata as self-evident.

I have sometimes jokingly said that defining "meta" is like defining another four-letter word, "porn": you know it when you see it. But this parallel is surprisingly accurate, because what is widely understood with regard to the obscene—but almost never acknowledged with regard to the meta- prefix—is that both are (like all social phenomena) defined by communities of practice. What counts as obscenity depends on the norms of a particular time and place; what counts as "meta" is similarly contextual. In linguistic terms, it is misleading to seek a parallel between the zero-degree and the meta in terms of a structural distinction like that between speech and grammar. It is more effective to think in terms of "codeswitching" between English and Spanish, the movement between formal and informal registers of a language, or even "tagging"—understood as emergent acts of labeling that become generally accepted "hashtag" categories over time.

Consider how search terms, a prototypical example of "metadata," can become "data" through social practice. This happens when such searches are (often inaccurately) used to track possible influenza outbreaks. Another example of this—discussed by the internet scholar Tarleton Gillespie among others—occurred when LGBT activists responded to the heterosexist stance of former Pennsylvania congressman Rick Santorum by using his name as part of a search string for sexual fluids, temporarily pushing a "spreadingsantorum.com" Web site created by activists to first place in Google's results for the term "santorum." In instances like these, phenomena typically classed as metacommunication act as forms of communication.

This is perhaps the most important theoretical issue with regard to the making of metadata, one with implications for social theory more generally. The fact that the act of "meta" assignment is culturally contextual is relevant to any use of the prefix, from metaphysics to metapragmatics, from metacommunication to metamedia, from metaknowledge to metaculture. Indeed, Gregory Bateson—one of the classic anthropologists most cited by scholars of communication and digital culture—theorized in his article "A Theory of Play and Fantasy" that these forms of metacommunication were crucial to the evolution of communication itself, since they marked a threshold for recognizing that the "signals" of communication are "signals" at all. A better understanding of the making of *meta-* will therefore be central to understanding emerging forms of big data and their social implications.

The dialectic of surveillance and recognition

The Snowden affair magnified existing debates regarding big data, surveillance and state power. In turn, these debates clearly draw from a contested cultural logic of monitoring, privacy and disclosure. My tentative name for this logic is "the dialectic of surveillance and recognition," and this speaks to Bell's provocation regarding how data "loves a good relationship."

Snowden's revelations of big-data-enabled state surveillance left many grasping for precedents, analogues, metaphors. One of the most common was "Orwellian," but many found this a limited trope because it failed to capture how the "big data" concept includes both relatively non-intentional data (like GPS data generated by a moving cellphone) and relatively intentional data (like a Facebook posting).

Perhaps this is why Snowden invoked not George Orwell but Michel Foucault: "if a surveillance program produces information of value, it legitimizes it....In one step, we've managed to justify the operation of the Panopticon." Snowden here referenced Foucault's discussion in *Discipline and Punish* of the Panopticon, proposed by the utilitarian philosopher Jeremy Bentham as part of prison reform. A prison would be composed of cells facing a central tower, the Panopticon, allowing a single guard to monitor the prison. Furthermore, the Panopticon would be designed so that prisoners could never tell if someone was in the tower. They would internalize the Panopticon's gaze and monitor their own behavior.

However, from a Foucauldian perspective the master metaphor for making big data should not be the Panopticon, but the confession. While published only one year after *Discipline and Punish* and sharing many themes with that earlier work, in *The History of Sexuality, Volume 1* Foucault turned even greater attention to how power, knowledge and selfhood come together in specific historical contexts. In a chapter titled "The Incitement to Discourse," he traced the emergence of "a political, economic, and technical incitement to talk about sex...in the form of analysis, stocktaking, classification, and specification, of quantitative or causal studies" (page 23–24). Sex was *made into data*, with two crucial implications. First, that data was part of a state project. Second, this data was produced through a "confessional" discourse drawing from Christianity and the psychoanalytic encounter between therapist and patient.

The confession is a modern mode of making data, an incitement to discourse we might now term an *incitement to disclose*. It is profoundly dialogical: one confesses to a powerful Other. To further address how this incitement to disclose plays out in contemporary contexts, it will be helpful to consider Charles Taylor's well-known essay "The politics of recognition" (1994). Here, Taylor identified as a key aspect of modernity the assumption that one's identity is shaped by the recognition of others, so that an inaccurate or biased conception could cause "real damage" to the person or community so misrecognized.

In speaking of the "dialectic of surveillance and recognition," I seek to link the notion of confessional discourse to the politics of recognition. A thesis for further research is that the rise of big data is accompanied by a discourse that links surveillance to recognition, that *frames surveillance as a form of belonging*. No discourse is singular and there are certainly reverse discourses, counterdiscourses and alternate discourses. At issue is not that the kind of state surveillance highlighted by the Snowden affair is uncontested (because it obviously is contested), but understanding how so many find surveillance acceptable and even pleasurable. One of the most important political lessons of Foucault's work was the insight that resistance often emerges from within a discourse in a complex fashion poorly represented by purist notions of oppositionality. With regard to queer politics, Foucault noted in *The History of Sexuality* that the mid-nineteenth century pathological understanding of homosexuality

> [m]ade possible the formation of a "reverse" discourse: homosexuality began to speak in its own behalf, to demand that its legitimacy or "naturality" be acknowledged, often in the same vocabulary, using the same categories by which it was medically disqualified.

It is not yet clear what kind of reverse discourses will emerge with regard to big data and its dialectic of surveillance and recognition. However, one clue can be seen in the fact that many responses to the making of big data are implicitly calls not for its abolition, but its extension. Many critics of big data question the biases that occur when certain communities (usually those with less resources) are not counted or included in big data analytics. I share this concern that more people be included. The point is that in an almost homeopathic fashion, the remedy lies within the conceptual horizon of the illness it is to mitigate—within the dialectic of surveillance and recognition.

Rotted data, thick data

Snowden justified his revelations of NSA surveillance by arguing such data collection always takes place in an interpretive frame—even one applied after the fact, so that a government could "go back in time and scrutinize every decision you've ever made." He thus linked claims about data and temporality to "scrutiny"—to the culturally contextual work of interpretation. This echoes an emerging literature challenging the notion of "raw" data, a notion that should be of interest to anthropologists given its reference to Claude Lévi-Strauss's *The Raw and the Cooked*, published in 1969.

Strikingly, this binarism of raw/cooked is both etic (an outsider framework) and emic (used in everyday practice). These categories are incredibly important with regard to big data. One reason is the implication that the "bigness" of data means it must be collected prior to interpretation—"raw." This is revealed by metaphors like data "scraping" that suggest scraping flesh from bone, removing something taken as a self-evidently surface phenomenon. Another implication is that in a brave new world of big data, the interpretation of that data—its "cooking"—will increasingly be performed by computers themselves.

Yet this is another instance where classic anthropological work provides insight. While Lévi-Strauss often treated the raw and cooked in a dichotomous fashion, in "The culinary triangle," published one year after *The Raw and the Cooked*, he placed these categories in a triadic relationship with the "rotted." In this full theorization, "raw" and "cooked" are not set in a binary where raw = nature and cooked = culture. Instead, they are framed as elements of a "culinary triangle" shaped by the intersection of the binarisms of nature/culture and normal/transformed (Figure 1).

This trichotomy holds stimulating potential for theorizing the making of big data. Like "raw" and "cooked," the category of the "rotted" is emic as well as etic, as seen in the notion of "bit rot." This can refer to the materiality of data—the way that decaying computer tape and damaged hard drives cause data loss. The "rotted" allows for transformations outside typical constructions of the human agent as cook—the unplanned, unexpected and accidental. Bit rot, for instance, emerges from the assemblage of storage and

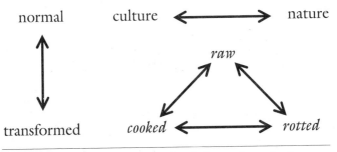

Figure 1: Lévi-Strauss's culinary triangle (image by author).

processing technologies as they move through time. But "rotting" moves between nature and society as well as between intentional and unintentional. Lévi-Strauss himself noted that rotting can be "either spontaneous or controlled;" in the latter case it is often termed "fermentation" or "distillation" and produces everything from bread and cheese to beer and wine.

Given longstanding notions of "distilling" meaning from big data, the notion of rotted data might thereby provide a conceptual lens to consider imbrications of the intentional and random in the generation, interpretation and application of big data. A "culinary data triangle" places raw and cooked in a logical rather than temporal relation. With three terms in a triangle rather than two terms in a row it is easier to avoid imputing a timeline. It is easier to avoid assuming that the raw comes before the cooked, and thus easier to challenge the claim to power embedded in the temporal argument that data comes before interpretation. A notion of "rotted data" reflects how data can be transformed in parahuman, complexly material and temporally emergent ways that do not always follow a preordained, algorithmic "recipe." In Bell's words, it gives us tools for considering how data can be "messy" and even resist being "tidied up."

It is possible to build on classic anthropological insights beyond those of Lévi-Strauss. In challenging the notion of "raw data," many scholars have emphasized the importance of interpretation, which recalls Clifford Geertz's classic intervention into another debate over making data. In his article "Thick description: Toward an interpretive theory of culture," Geertz responded to cognitive anthropologists like Ward Goodenough and Charles Frake, whose scholarship in turn contributed to the algorithmic frameworks central to contemporary big data. Geertz built on the philosopher Gilbert Ryle's notion of "thick description," which Ryle illustrated by noting the difference between twitching one's eye in an involuntary manner on the one hand, and on the other winking at someone. The "data" is identical, but the meaning is vastly different, based on a plane of public, shared meaning.

In placing Lévi-Strauss and Geertz into conversation with contemporary debates regarding "raw data," I mean neither to reduce them to each other nor claim that they provide a solution. Instead, like the notion of "metadata," the notion of "raw data" demands an ongoing theoretical response. A valuable part of that response can be rethinking rhetorics of the unprecedented and accelerated that imply we have nothing to learn from the history of social theory. Against the "thin" notion of raw data, we can think of data not just as cooked or rotted but "thick." This highlights how big data is never ontologically prior to interpretation, and interpretation takes place within horizons of culture that are embedded in contexts of power.

Conclusion: making up big data

In this piece, I have sought to open up multiple lines of inquiry with regard to the making of big data. Building on a range of scholarly conversations, I have explored temporality and the possibilities of "dated theory," the implicit histories shaping metadata, "the dialectic of surveillance and recognition," and questions of interpretation understood in terms of "rotted data" and "thick data." The goal has been to expand frameworks for addressing issues of time, context and power. As an ethnographer I appreciate the value of focused and localized explanation, but we cannot cede more generalized theorizing to only some disciplines and methodological approaches. There is a need for what I term "platform-agnostic theory"—for theories that make claims about patterns and dynamics beyond the case study and the individual field site, even as those specificities shape the building of theory as well as its contextual modification.

Big data represents more than "scrapes" of reality—it is part and parcel of that reality, immanent to the human condition. Big data is always already "big theory" as well, acknowledged or not. How these informational regimes shape societies into the emerging future depends in no small measure on our ability to understand and respond to the making up of big data itself. ■

Also available from Prickly Paradigm Press:

continued

continued